English naive painting
1750 - 1900

JAMES AYRES

Preface by
ANDRAS KALMAN

with 151 illustrations,
48 in colour

THAMES AND HUDSON

For Peter

Filmset in Great Britain by Keyspools Ltd, Golborne, Lancs
Printed and Bound in the Netherlands by
Smeets B. V. Weert

Contents

Acknowledgments

Public collections in Britain contain few examples of indigenous naive painting. Indeed, in the preparation of this book some institutions denied ownership of paintings they were known to possess, although they were always most helpful in granting reproduction rights. By default, private collections have provided the principal material for this book. Among these the collection formed by the late John Judkyn is represented through the courtesy of Dr Dallas Pratt, and paintings from the Kalman Collection by courtesy of Mr and Mrs Andras Kalman. I would also like to pay a special tribute to Mr Christopher Bibby for providing photographs of pictures which have been through his hands. Many other private collectors have been most helpful, especially Mr and Mrs Roger Bichard, Mr and Mrs Andrew Jenkins, Mr Ian McCallum, Mr and Mrs Derek Balmer, and Mr and Mrs Michael Reeves.

Also included are reproductions of pictures from the Royal Scottish Academy, Blackburn Museum and Art Gallery, Blaise Castle House Folk Museum at Henbury, Bristol, the Herbert Art Gallery and Museum, Coventry, Luton Museum and Art Gallery, the National Museum of Wales in Cardiff, Central Museum and Art Gallery, Northampton, Tate Gallery, London, Tunbridge Wells Municipal Museum and Art Gallery, and the Victoria and Albert Museum, London.

In recognition of the personal help received from the staff of museums and art galleries, I have pleasure in thanking Beatrix Rumford (Abby Aldrich Rockefeller Folk Art Collection, Williamsburg), Katherine Eustace, Arnold Wilson and Francis Greenacre (Bristol City Art Gallery), Michael Day (Norfolk Museums Service), Margaret Fuller and Sadie Ward (Museum of English Rural Life, Reading), and Jane Evans (Woodspring Museum, Weston-Super-Mare). I am indebted to David Addison (Cheltenham Art Gallery and Museum) and J. F. Rhodes (City Museum and Art Gallery, Gloucester) for information on J. Miles of Northleach; to Antonia Roberts (Rochdale Museum and Art Gallery) for details on John Collier; and to Jenny Spencer-Smith (National Army Museum, London) for information on naive watercolour portraits of British soldiers. The photograph of a *Nocturne* by Walter Greaves was obtained through Pamela Reekie of the Hunterian Museum, Glasgow, and information on J. W. H. Southby (as well as the photograph of his painting) was obtained through the generous help of Canon George Youell, Vice Dean of Ely Cathedral.

Identification of the livestock in some of the paintings was made by Mrs Anne George and Mr Joe Henson of the Cotswold Farm Park (Rare Breeds Survival Centre). Finally, I am indebted to Sarah Trevatt for maintaining the book file, and to my wife Annabel for helping to prepare this manuscript.

Bath, October 1979   JAMES AYRES

6

Preface

Folk art is the 'endangered species' of the English art world. It is diminishing, and no 'reservation' has been created for its survival.

Art historians, writing in glossy art magazines and museum journals, are inclined to focus considerable attention on some seventeenth-century Italian or Flemish painter, quoting one another's writings in endless, pompous appendixes. The more numerous these are, the more learned the thesis appears to be. But no university curriculum includes English folk art and naive painting. Hardly a book on the history of English art mentions the subject. No curators or students research it. Yet folk or naive art is related to the most English of art: to the work of Hogarth, Wootton, Rowlandson, the superb Stubbs, the underrated Seymour, the near-naive Devis, to Dadd, to Lowry and Stanley Spencer of our own time. Perhaps even to the young Gainsborough.

The study of English art is overweight with its classical legacy. It has thwarted interest in the heritage of ordinary people: seamen, farmers, innkeepers, tradesmen, village parsons, artisans.

Of course they had their art too! They made carvings, bold shop signs, pictures in paint and other media, colourful embroideries, amusing pottery, and beautiful, austere furniture. But in the Age of Elegance who cared for this simple, earthy art, an art without pedigree? Fine art was the realm of the aristocracy, part of whose education consisted of the Grand Tour of Europe. Scholars followed the upper classes in pursuit of classicism, and created a barrier in English art which persists to this day. The Italian palazzos with marble floors, gilded furniture, portraits in massive, carved frames, left a profound impression on the English visitors.

The increasing wealth of England's ruling class made it possible to invite architects and craftsmen from Italy and elsewhere, a process beginning as early as Holbein, and including Van Dyck, Rubens,

Canaletto and many others. But in social terms the classes mingled mostly on the sporting field. They wagered together at races, boxing matches, cockfights, bear baitings; and these sports were frequently recorded for the great houses by trained and skilled artists, and for the yeoman farmer or innkeeper by travelling craftsmen. So it was likely that the pictures by Wootton, Stubbs or Canaletto were passed on with the cautionary words, 'Look after these. They are art treasures!' No such warning was given for the preservation of modest folk art. Who would look after the works of itinerant artists? The innkeeper? He would of course keep an overmantel picture of, say, the London to Brighton stagecoach which called at his property. But what happened when, blackened with soot and cracked by heat, the panels ceased to be a decoration? As they were of no monetary value and not sought after by scholars, and no museums in the nineteenth century displayed them, many delightful examples of folk art just perished.

When I started to collect English folk art, I had the greatest difficulty in persuading professional restorers to save some of the time-ravaged canvases. The odd portrait would survive in good condition, a little girl on her pony, for instance. Perhaps it had been kept in a clean bedroom. Others, of sporting events, 'ship's likenesses', topographical subjects, may have become relegated to a spare room or attic, later to be bought by a few enthusiasts, mostly inspired by American folk art.

America, with a culture more recent and democratic than that of Europe, lacked a heavy classical inheritance in the arts, and therefore cherished its folk art. And how magnificent it is! One wishes it were seen more in England, for it is in this area that the strongest cultural affinity appears to exist between the two countries. In Spain (and Spanish America), Italy or France the folk artists tended to devote their talents to devotional works. Very many churches are decorated with their *ex-voto* (thanksgiving) pictures. In England and America they preferred to depict daily life, and did so with honesty, warmth and simplicity. These qualities, together with the childlike surprises and humour so abundant in folk and naive art, but rarely seen in academic art, enticed me into forming my collection.

ANDRAS KALMAN
London, October 1979

8

Introduction

Naive art, 1750–1900: towards a definition

THE ART DISCUSSED in this book is called 'naive', a word which carries associations of the 'primitive', the 'amateur', and the 'non-academic'. But it may in practice be sophisticated in technique, or civilized in terms of the context from whence it sprang, or professional as regards training and payment. Such art exists at many levels, but all of them are outside the canons of taste established by the élite culture. In many ways 'vernacular' art – a word which has been usefully applied to architecture – would be a more appropriate term. 'Popular art', as part of 'popular culture', has come to mean something rather different, and because it includes the products of printing press and camera it is now all but confined to these media.

Because of the inadequacy of these terms some people may argue that no such species as 'naive art' exists, and that it is only the aesthetic uncertainties of the twentieth century that have led us to praise the inadequate as naive. No wonder, the argument could run, it took a period such as ours to hail the work of the French customs official Rousseau and the English ship's chandler Alfred Wallis. At a slightly earlier time such painters would have been 'corrected' out of their artistic existence, just as Whistler corrected or 'improved' the brothers Greaves.

The selection of paintings as naive often becomes a matter of subjective judgment rather than historical circumstance. In America Kenneth Ames has argued that folk art (often used interchangeably if not synonymously with naive art) should be seen as part of folk culture.[1] In Britain, if folk art is considered at all it is often viewed only as part of folk culture. Another American, Henry Glassie, is like Ames inclined to the suspect view that folk art is the product of amateurs. However, there is much to be said for Glassie's opinion that 'most of "folk" art is not "folk" because it is "popular"; the paintings made on velvet by young ladies in seminaries and academies for example.'[2]

The notion that the practice of art was a popular pursuit of the élite may be ancient. Stalker and Parker, in order to promote sales of their book in the 'right' quarters, proclaimed:

The Grecians . . . had so great an honour for this Art, that they ordained, That Gentlemen's Sons and Freeborn should be first sent to a Painting-School, to learn the way to Paint and Draw Pictures, before they were instructed in any other thing; Slaves and vulgar hands, by perpetual Edict, were excluded from the benefit and practice of it.[3]

The historical truth of this statement is less important than the prejudices it reveals. Today, with our more proletarian aspirations, the exceptions assume a sociological importance that unconsciously affects the eye. We are predisposed to like the work that was conceived and born in the egalitarian circumstances of a craftsman/painter producing pictures which, unlike child art, show an experience of life largely innocent of the prejudices which both formed and isolated the élite culture.

Doubtless the appreciation of such works does much to illuminate twentieth-century art and art history. It would however be quite wrong to conclude that such non-academic work has been identified retrospectively, or that it did not have a separate existence in its own day. Eighteenth- and nineteenth-century trade directories customarily list exponents of the 'polite arts' under the heading 'Artists, Portrait, Landscape, Miniature.' However, another category of painter may also be found listed under 'Painters, House, Sign &c.' Fortunately some of these painters signed their work, and in at least one instance it has been possible to prove that a professional painter of this type is listed under 'Plumbers & Glaziers' with 'artist and painter' added after his name. Clearly such individuals regarded themselves, and were regarded by others, as quite distinct from their contemporaries who termed themselves 'Artists'.

Because the position of the 'vernacular' artist was of a different order from that of the academic painter, the work that he produced was based upon tenets less consciously held but which were none the less distinctive for that. The modern cult of the individual with its roots in humanism and the Renaissance was not part of his mental baggage, for the vernacular artist was a man of a still older tradition where originality was not everything. Just as the medieval craftsman/painter might use a manuscript herbal as the basis for a detail in a panel painting, so these journeymen/ painters of the eighteenth and nineteenth centuries, the spiritual and technical descendants of the medieval craftsmen, would lift details and often whole compositions from printed sources. Edward Hicks, perhaps the best known of all American naive painters, derived all his work (with the exception of a couple of 'farm-scapes') from sources other than his own imagination, observation or knowledge. Perhaps he is referring to his use of engravings when he makes the following observation in one of the rhymes quoted in his autobiography:

Inferior folks with only monkey's art,

May imitate but never life impart.

Obvious originality is a tyranny which has emerged in the twentieth century. Despite the fact that he often took his material from printed sources, the naive artist achieved originality through an earthy native genius. This 'genius' may not represent a great sweep of philosophical thought but, where it exists, it has the instinctive power to provide enjoyment for the unprejudiced spectator. What then are the identifiable qualities of this genius?

At times, of course, these vernacular artists display a technical virtuosity over the preparation and use of materials, both pigment and media, in which they may surpass their more fashionable contemporaries. The disastrous use of bitumen by Sir Joshua Reynolds springs to mind. Furthermore, in the drawing of the human figure they ignored the rules of classical proportion so that the portraits that they painted have a directness and are never 'dated' if always datable. In the representation of animals these artists' closeness to the earth gives their best pictures the mystical power of true observation, informed by memory based on long experience, which is reminiscent of the cave paintings of Altamira and Lascaux. An understanding of tonal recession or of optical perspective is often rudimentary or non-existent, but indeed such considerations are frequently unimportant. A sailor would want to see both prow and stern of his ship; a townscape or an estate painting would be expected to illustrate both plan and elevation, and these artists were quite prepared to distort the optical facts in order to demonstrate the greater truth of the memory's eye. For this reason reflected colour and light are absent, and objective rather than observed facts are displayed with a heraldic power uncorrupted by the effects of their surroundings: a white cow *in* a green field is a white cow *on* a green field. The absence of perspective which maintains the respect for the picture plane, and the use of pungent colour and powerful form, are features which serve to emphasize the great abilities often possessed by these artists in orchestrating such strong and usually contradictory elements in their compositions. The cumulative effect of these various virtues in the hands of a painter with an innate 'eye' results in a canvas, panel or assemblage in which virtuosity is always subordinate to the subject.

It is disturbing that the English have been slow to recognize the sophistication to be found in the so-called naive paintings of the past. Such objects were made for the most part by painters whose income from their craft was not large at a time when leisure was an indulgence enjoyed by only a few. What better evidence could there be to suggest that art is a necessity for all?

Decline or evolution?

With the commercial appearance of photography in 1839 many painters were to lose their clientele. Some attempted to combine the skills of painting with those of the camera but, predictably, photography was to dominate. There were also other innovations that were to have their impact, in particular the products of the printing press. Black and white engravings had long been available but it was the development of the colour print that made them truly competitive. As early as 1836 Loudon was able to state that 'there is no cottage or dwelling, however humble, in which there will not be found some object purely ornamental . . .' He goes on to observe that 'engravings of the rudest kinds' were to be found even in 'the most wretched log houses in Russia.'[4] By 1872 John Frost of Clare Street, Bristol, was but one of many throughout the country who could supply 'Oleographs, Fac-simile oil paintings' and the 'best selection of Chromographs, imitating watercolours. . .'[5]

Changing social patterns brought about by the industrial revolution also had their impact upon the naive artist and his work. In some instances these changes encouraged and inspired the development of new traditions in vernacular painting. The roses and castles of the narrowboat are an example, a late flowering that oddly enough did not begin until the canals themselves were in decline due to competition with the railways. So long as the canals were a commercial success they were operated by men whose homes were land-based and whose boats bore little or no decoration beyond a name, number and possibly a heart, club, diamond or spade. When the canals began their decline in the 1830s the canal boats could only be a paying proposition if families lived aboard and provided free labour. Once the narrowboat became a home it evolved its own inimitable decoration.

In the second half of the nineteenth century, when serious thought was given to housing and education for all, it was perhaps inevitable that the new paternalism would destroy much that was valuable. The attitudes that were adopted towards naive artists of various periods are symptomatic of these changes. George Smart of Frant was certainly not ignored by his early nineteenth-century contemporaries, but neither do they seem to have felt any need to 'improve' him. The same cannot be said of Walter Greaves

61   of Chelsea whose *Hammersmith Bridge on Boat-Race Day* has been described as 'Britain's greatest naive painting'.[6] It was made in 1862 when Walter Greaves was only sixteen years of age. The following year (most authorities agree) Greaves met a new neighbour – the American painter, James McNeill Whistler. Never again did Greaves produce such a fine painting. In his youth he achieved an instinctive sophistication. In contrast the work of his maturity was either of the level of a worthy amateur or simply a

62   pastiche of Whistler's *Nocturnes.*

In the late 1920s conventionally trained artists were developing a profound respect for the work of naive painters whose native condition was preserved by what may be described as a more anthropological approach. Indeed, far from attempting to 'improve' such an artist, Christopher Wood (1901–30) on occasion went so far as to imitate the work of Alfred Wallis. Wood, for all his academic training, was not informed by Wallis's background, and by impersonating his idiom he trivialized his own undoubted gifts. Perhaps more painters than we may suspect have been influenced, if not directly by naive artists, then indirectly by a sentiment of our time which responds to those qualities which are instinctively arrived at by the vernacular painter. In looking at the pictures on the following pages some may see a Hockney in *A Foreign Port*, a Lowry in Wainwright's *Yorkshire Street Corner*, a James Lloyd in Joseph Sheppard's *Captain Scarlet* or a David Inshaw in Herbert Rylance's view of a Coventry park. Although the reader may disagree with many of these comparisons it will doubtless be disconcerting for some to see how the once ridiculed naive artists anticipated the work of our own contemporaries.

130
38
107
41

Many painters working today in a supposedly innocent idiom are not, whatever else they may be, naive. The whole area abounds with confusion. In an attempt to map this chaotic field Eric Lister and Sheldon Williams have identified eight categories of twentieth-century naive painting, including 'Naive Innocents', 'Naive Fantasists' and 'Naive Sophisticates', which somehow compound the problem.[7] In 1979 the Arts Council of Great Britain staged an exhibition entitled '*Outsiders*: an art without precedent or tradition'. This miscellaneous collection of the work of mental patients and amateurs, as well as of trained artists, points to the possibility that there exists an 'alternative art' outside the canons of taste (no longer established by academies) which results from the actions of grant-giving agencies of the State such as Arts Councils or National Endowments.

As soon as naive art was recognized its continued existence as a living art form was in jeopardy. A number of art historians have remarked on this. Oto Bihalji-Merin has stated that '*naive art* which takes notice of the temptations of the market whether in Paris or Hlebine, New York or Haiti, always runs the risk of forsaking the true climate of its existence.'[8] In fact, as Klaus Jurgen-Fischer perceptively remarked at the 1970 Hlebine Symposium, 'It [naive art] has lost its innocence, and is in danger of developing into an academy of amateurism . . .'[9]

In a country as large as the United States, genuinely naive artists uninformed by the cynicism of our time may yet persist uncorrupted.[10] They have undoubtedly been subjected to the information explosion dispensed by television, but they may not have eaten of the Tree of Knowledge. In Britain that Garden of Eden is no more, which is why the fruits of its naivety are so compelling.

Painters and their customers

The 'itinerant limner' is a personage who has attracted some interest, but how many of these craftsmen were itinerant, and how appropriate is the designation of 'limner'? In the eighteenth and certainly by the nineteenth century improved communications ensured that there were few parts of England so remote as to be beyond the reach of towns of sufficient consequence to support a few provincial artists, and the work of these men often achieved metropolitan standards; the Cornishman, John Opie, before his arrival in London, was just such an artist. The diffusion of these artistic standards throughout England would have deprived the itinerant artist of many potential customers. The peripatetic artist was probably more a figure of the eighteenth century. The word 'limner' derives from *luminer*, one who illuminates manuscripts, and it long retained an association with miniatures in watercolour. William Salmon defined 'Limning' in his *Polygraphice* (1672) as 'an Art whereby in water Colours, we strive to resemble Nature in everything to the Life.' By the eighteenth century the word was not always used with precision,[11] as can be seen in Oliver Goldsmith's *The Vicar of Wakefield* (1766).[12] The vicar's neighbours, the Flamboroughs, 'had lately got their pictures drawn by a limner, who travelled the country, and took likenesses for fifteen shillings a head.' Not wishing to be outdone the vicar's family determined to have their own portraits 'taken':

. . . Our next deliberation was to show the superiority of our tastes in the attitudes. As for our neighbour's family there were seven of them and they were drawn with seven oranges – a thing quite out of taste, no variety in life, no composition in the world. We desired to have something in a brighter style; and, after many debates, at length came to a unanimous resolution of being drawn together in one large historical piece. This would be cheaper, since one frame would serve for all, and it would be infinitely more genteel; for all families of any taste were now drawn in the same manner. As we did not immediately recollect an historical subject to hit us, we were contented each with being drawn as independent historical figures. My wife desired to be represented as Venus, and the painter was desired not to be too frugal of his diamonds on her stomacher and hair. Her little ones were to be as Cupids by her side; while I, in my gown and band, was to present her with my books on the Whistonian controversy. Olivia would be drawn as an Amazon, sitting upon a bank of flowers dressed in a green joseph, richly laced in gold, and a whip in her hand. Sophia was to be a shepherdess, with as many sheep as the painter could put in for nothing; and Moses was to be dressed out with a hat and a white feather. Our taste so much pleased the 'Squire, that he insisted on being put in as one of the family, in the character of Alexander the Great, at Olivia's feet. This was considered by us all as an indication of his desire to be introduced into the family, nor could we refuse his request. The painter was therefore set to work, and, as he wrought with assiduity and expedition, in less than four days the whole was completed. The piece was large, and, it must be owned, he did not spare his colours; for which my wife gave him great encomiums. We were all perfectly satisfied with his performance; but an unfortunate circumstance had not occurred till the picture was finished, which now struck us with dismay. It was so very large, that we had no place in the house to fix it . . . The picture therefore instead of gratifying our vanity, as we hoped, leaned, in a most mortifying manner against the kitchen wall, where the canvas was stretched and painted, much too large to be got through any of the doors, and the jest of all our neighbours . . .

By the nineteenth century provincial artists were very much town-based, although they would work within a twenty-five mile radius of their permanent address. The trade directories abound with the names of such individuals. Characteristic of these was the Walters family of Bristol who generally described themselves as 'Ornamental Painters' under the general heading 'Painters, House, Sign &c', in contrast to those who styled themselves 'Artists'. The latter category contained, in Pigot's *Directory* for Bristol in 1830, no less than eight names including 'Rippingale Alexander (miniature) 8 Lower crescent'. The Walters family is listed as follows:[13]

1819	Walter Thomas, Sign & Furniture Painter, 1 Lower College Street
1821	Walters Thos., Sign & Furniture Painter, St John's Bridge
1823	Walters Thos., Ornamental Sign Painter, 94 Old Market Street
1824	Walters Thos., Ornamental Sign Painter, 94 Old Market Street
1826–31	Walters Thos., Sign & Ornamental Painter, 16 Upper Maudlin Street
1831	Walters Thos. & Sons, Sign & Ornamental Painters, 16 Upper Maudlin Street
1832	Walters Thos., Sign & Ornamental Painter, 15 Narrow Wine Street Walters Geo., Ornamental Painted Baize manufacturer for table covers, mats, etc, 15 Narrow Wine Street
1834	*Not mentioned*
1835–8	Walters & Son, Painters, 26 Upper Maudlin Street
1844–7	Walters T., House & Ornamental Painter, 26 Upper Maudlin Street
1847	Walters G. T., Decorative & pictorial artist, grainer, gilder, and paper hanger, 26 Upper Maudlin Street

A shipping picture dated 1827 is signed 'Walters' (presumably Thomas) and shows *The William Miles of Bristol*.[14] Recently two large murals of *c.* 1835 signed 'Walters' (probably Walters & Son) have come to light at Phippens Farm, Butcombe, near Blagdon, about ten miles south of Bristol. These murals are painted in the manner of the scenic wallpapers which were so popular at this time. Due to the tax on paper the printed wallpapers were more expensive and therefore more fashionable than the hand-painted murals by craftsmen such as Walters.[15]

122

In a city the size of London the versatility required of craftsmen in provincial towns was absent. Pigot's *Commercial Directory* for London for the years 1823–4 lists under 'Painters, Plumbers and Glaziers' no less than eleven firms whose names were identified by means of an asterisk as 'Ornamental Painters'.

Small towns were of course much less well served by tradesmen of all descriptions. Pigot's *Directory* for Rugby of 1835 lists neither 'Artists' nor 'Painters, House, Sign &c'. However, under 'Plumbers and Glaziers' may be found 'Bagshaw Wm. (& painter)'. The oil paintings of

111, 112 a *White Ram* and a *White Ewe* are thus far the only identified works of this man, who may be regarded as a semi-professional artist. In towns with a still smaller population, craftsmen would frequently extend their skills to include the production of pictures. George Smart, a tailor by trade in the village of Frant near Tunbridge Wells, was just such an individual, successfully selling his feltwork collages to people of fashion who visited the spa to take the waters. A guide to the spa, W. Kidd's *Pocket Companion* (*c.* 1830), refers to Smart as follows:

While at Frant, it would be inexcusable not to visit Mr Smart, the far famed *taylor*, who, however *humble* his situation in life may appear, we consider worthy of a very honourable mention in this place. To quote his own words, he is, in addition to his *profession*, 'artist in cloth and velvet figures to His Royal Highness the Duke of Sussex'. These figures are admirably executed, more particularly old Bright, the postman many years sweeper of Tunbridge Wells walks. From my judge of Mr Smart's capabilities as an artist Mr S. is a poet, as may be seen from the following, taken, *by permission*, of course, from his album.

142 The verse that Smart used on his trade label (reproduced on page 148) is then quoted, the last line of which reads, 'And you may purchase if inclin'd'. The *Pocket Companion* continues with heavy irony:

The hint thrown out in the last line is generally taken, few persons visiting the place, without providing themselves with a *memento* of this singular, eccentric, but good humoured taylor – we ask his pardon – '*artist*'.

In general Smart seems to have relied on his own capabilities as a

141 draftsman. His representation of *The Goosewoman*, Elizabeth Horne, bears no relationship to C. Hulton's lithograph which was made in 1830, when

the subject was aged eighty-eight. However, Smart was not above plagiarizing himself, and his more popular subjects were virtually mass produced. His most successful and certainly his most amusing production was *The Earth Stopper* (one who stopped up foxes' earths the night before the hunt). Early examples usually bear a hand-written description pasted to the back of the frame, but he later used a label printed by Clifford of Tunbridge Wells, indicating that Smart was producing these pictures in quite large numbers. *The Earth Stopper* is perhaps the only example of Smart's work that is adapted in part from an engraved source, for it resembles Nathan Drake's *The Earth Stopper*, engraved by V. Green in 1767.[16]

92

The use of engravings by naive painters was probably quite general, but occasionally examples of such pirating occur in the opposite direction. Those who organized voyages of exploration and discovery would sometimes recommend the inclusion of artists to record what was seen. Among these 'artists of record' were the sixteenth-century Frenchman, Jacques le Moyne, and his English painter/stainer contemporary, John White. Anson, in his *Voyage Round the World* (1748), suggested that officers with 'proficiency in drawing' should sail on men-of-war, a recommendation that was later accepted by the Admiralty.[17] Professional landscape and botanical artists accompanied Captain Cook on his three voyages. After the deaths of Buchan and Parkinson in the course of the first voyage the paintings and drawings by seamen became the only available record. One in the author's collection, *The Inside of a Hippah* [Maori village], *in New Zealand*, which was later copied by Webber and engraved by Rennoldson, is an example. The process by which this picture moved up the social scale of art helps to establish the distinctions between the different levels of naive art, as well as its area of definition. The original painting by an anonymous seaman – possibly Cook himself – has all the immediacy of actual observation of simple Maori people and volcanic mountains. John Webber's watercolour[18] and the engraving which follows it not only show less of the village but have all the symptoms of the classically trained eye in the treatment of the human figures, whilst the mountain in the background obviously derives from European examples.

The relationship between engraving and painting at the vernacular level

11   is illustrated in the work of John Kay of Edinburgh (1742–1826), a barber by training who worked both as a miniature painter and as an engraver, thanks to the financial independence given him by his patron, William Nisbet of Dirleton. Typically, his work was in the past dismissed because 'being entirely self taught Kay's work is of negligible artistic merit'.[19] In northern England at a rather earlier date John Collier (1708–86)

5, 6   developed a considerable reputation as a painter, engraver and writer.[20] His father, a humble curate, had intended him for the church. When the elder Collier suddenly became blind at the early age of forty his son was apprenticed to a Dutch-loom weaver at Newton Moor, Mottram, near Manchester. But after little more than a year he persuaded his master to cancel his indentures. He became an itinerant schoolmaster and was appointed sub-master of the free school at Milnrow, near Rochdale, in 1729, and ten years later became the master of the school, a job he retained until his death in 1786. Like Kay his development as an artist (and in Collier's case as a writer also) depended upon a patron. Collier's patron whilst at Milnrow was Colonel Richard Townley of Belfield, whose biography of his protégé was first published in the 1806 edition of *The Miscellaneous Works of Tim Bobbin*. Townley asserts that Collier's landscapes were drawn in 'good taste, understanding the rules of perspective, and some heads in profile with very decent success.'[21] C. W. Sutton, his biographer in the *Dictionary of National Biography*, states that he abandoned 'serious painting' for caricature, and that he turned to producing

> . . . a large number of grotesque pictures of buffoons, and hideous old women, painted in a style which is absolutely devoid of merit. They found a ready sale in the north of England and many specimens were until lately to be met with, chiefly in the drinking-rooms of old public-houses. He came to be styled the Lancashire Hogarth, but the designation is inappropriate. He turned his hand occasionally to carriage and sign painting, and to gravestone carving, as well as to land surveying at which he was expert.

Such condescension shows that naive painting was identified as such before it was enjoyed outside its own *milieu*. Gray's reference in his *Elegy* to 'uncouth rhimes and shapeless sculpture' is but an unenthusiastic recognition of folk poetry and naive sculpture. However, the vigour of

20

the non-academic tradition was constantly injecting life into the world of 'acceptable' art. Indeed, many academic artists began their careers as painter/craftsmen whose stock-in-trade included sign painting and the rendering of coats of arms on carriages and funeral hatchments. Among these craftsmen who later achieved fame in the 'polite arts' J. T. Smith mentions the Anglo-Swiss artist, Zoffany, who painted clock dials; Charles Catton RA (1728–98), 'in early life a coach and sign painter'; John Baker RA (1731–71), 'a famous Flower-painter, [who] decorated coach-panels with borders and wreaths of flowers'; and 'Clarkson, the portrait painter, [who] was originally a coach panel and sign painter and [who] executed a most elaborate one of Shakespeare which formerly hung across the street at the north east corner of Little Russell Street [but Edward] Edwards has erroneously given [Samuel] Wale the credit of the sign.'[22] Larwood and Hotten[23] state that 'Peter Monamy was apprenticed to a sign and house painter on London Bridge', and Robert Dalton served his time as an apprentice to a sign and coach painter, as did Ralph Kirby, Thomas Wright of Liverpool and Richard Smirke RA (1778–1815). The easel paintings by these men were not always admired by their contemporaries. Edward Edwards considered that John Baker's work was 'too much marked by that sharpness of touch, which is peculiar to all those who have been bred coach painters', whilst he totally dismissed the work of Richard Roper and George Evans.

The History of Signboards refers to a number of artists who were prepared to paint signs, among them David Cox, the elder Crome, George Henry Harlow, Julius Caesar Ibbetson, John Everett Millais, Charles Ross, Richard Wilson, and above all William Hogarth and George Moreland. In general, of course, painted and carved signs were made by humble craftsmen who in London seem to have been principally located at Harp Alley, Shoe Lane (off Fleet Street). Among these was Thomas Proctor 'at the Black-a-Moor's Head *in* Harp-Alley near Fleet-Ditch', whose trade label describes him as a '*Painter* who Painteth and Selleth all sorts of *Signs, Bushes, Bacchus's, Bunches* of *Grapes* and *Show-Boards*, at Reasonable Prices. The Oldest Shop.'[24] Some sign painters achieved a considerable measure of respect: 'Among the most celebrated practitioners in this branch was a person of the name of Lamb, who possessed considerable ability. His pencil was bold and masterly, and well adapted to the subjects on which it was generally employed. There was also Gwynne, another coach painter, who acquired some reputation as a marine painter, and produced a few good signs.'[25] The example of Gwynne is important, for it suggests that such a painter was able to work on large scale exterior work as well as at the more intimate level demanded of an easel painting designed to be hung indoors.

Most of the paintings illustrated in this book were made by professionals whose craft often exceeded their formal aesthetic training. Dickens's Miss La Creevy in *Nicholas Nickleby* (1839), is a typical example; portraiture was her stock-in-trade. From the late eighteenth century and on into the second half of the nineteenth, animal portraiture became a distinctive genre. This was occasioned by the development of agriculture in the late eighteenth century when the breeding of improved strains of livestock was developed seriously. Hitherto this interest, like the resulting paintings, had been almost exclusively concerned with horses and hounds. In the absence of bloodstock books cattle, sheep and pigs were reared to grotesque proportions so that each living specimen would testify to its unwritten pedigree. These animals of abnormal size and weight became sideshow spectacles and the subjects of paintings on which lithographs would be based, and these in turn generated further revenue for the breeders and owners. With the emergence of bloodstock books the practical need for such pictures declined, with inevitable deleterious effects upon the vigour of the tradition.

Kay of Edinburgh, Collier of Lancashire, Smart of Kent and others were all working men who abandoned their earlier careers to become artists working in two dimensions. The leisured classes, on the other hand, did not have to make such a difficult transition, and whereas most if not all professional or semi-professional vernacular artists were men, a great many amateur painters who came from the higher levels of society were women. As early as 1688 Stalker and Parker, in *A Treatise of Japaning and Varnishing*, had recommended lacquer work as a suitable pastime for women. In the eighteenth century shellwork became a fashionable activity, the most remarkable surviving example of which is a house with a hexadecagonal plan at Exmouth. Named *À la Ronde*, the interiors of this house built in 1795 are encrusted with shellwork and featherwork, all made by two spinster sisters named Parminster.

Occasionally, framed examples of this type of work will be found along with the more usual embroidered pictures. The designs were often derived from books of patterns printed expressly for the purpose, with titles like *The Ladies' Amusement* by Robert Sayer (1763) in which the engravings were by Jean Pillement.

It is just possible that materials other than paint were employed for artistic purposes because they were sometimes easier to use. The vicar's wife in *The Vicar of Wakefield* makes no reference to painting when she declares that

... my two daughters have a pretty good education ... They can read, write, and cast accounts, they understand their needle, broad stitch, cross and change, and all manner of plainwork; they can pink, point, and frill, and know something of music; they can do up small clothes, work upon catgut; my eldest can cut paper ...

Much of the skill – the craft basis underlying the 'art and mystery' of painting – was originally to be found in the preparation of pigment: 'The operation subservient to the making and preparing of colours [is] sublimation, calcination, solution, precipitation, filtration, and levigation,'[26] and on the addition of various media including, as well as the oils, size, wax and milk. In the eighteenth century Reeves & Son (founded in 1766) began the manufacture of watercolour cakes, and by the 1830s tube paints, both oil and watercolour, were in production. These innovations have been curiously ignored by art historians, and yet must rank in importance with the development of perspective in Renaissance Italy. Without such 'convenience paints' the objective study by artists of landscape and light in the open air would not have been possible. Furthermore, amateur painters did not emerge in great numbers until the daunting barrier of the craft of painting had been removed. Even then the trade directories show that 'Professors and Teachers' of drawing outnumbered teachers of painting six to one.[27] *The Female Student* (London, 1836)[28] went so far as to describe drawing as 'this accomplishment, so conducive to the refinement of the mind, [which] is at once useful and ornamental'. In addition to the young ladies in finishing schools, cadets in naval establishments and military academies were customarily taught drawing and painting to a very high order, since part of their professional work involved the recording of coastlines or enemy positions. No less an artist than Paul Sandby was the chief drawing-master at the Royal Military Academy, Woolwich.

Framing

So long as painting remained an architectural feature the movable picture frame was unimportant. When paintings ceased to be part of their physical environment the frame became a device whereby the picture could be isolated from its context and become an article of commerce to be hung in interiors of almost any character.

Some of the pictures illustrated in this book were originally part of panelled rooms and may be seen as marking the transition between paintings as architectural embellishment and paintings as independent art objects. Most characteristic of these are overmantel panels with surrounding bolection mouldings. In its architectural use the bolection moulding, in stone or wood, is a means whereby a higher plane, in this case the panel, may be connected to a lower one, in this case the stiles and rails. Accordingly, a painted overmantel panel framed by a bolection moulding is physically thrust forward. These mouldings were seldom carved (especially at the social level with which we are concerned) but they were often painted to simulate cedar-wood graining, marble or tortoiseshell. In paintings with considerable detail this counterfeit of exotic materials would have done much to enhance and draw attention to the picture by so 'distressing' the otherwise rather bald appearance of the moulding. This treatment was occasionally extended to other parts of the room. Wilsley House, Cranbrook, Kent, contains a late seventeenth- or early eighteenth-century room in which all the panels are framed-up in wood, painted to simulate marble. Every panel above the dado is painted with a shipping scene, and each of the lower panels shows a hound in pursuit of a hare (which is shown in the last panel). More accessible is an early eighteenth-century four-leaf screen in the Victoria and Albert Museum, in which each upper panel is painted with a woman emblematic of one of the four seasons with an appropriate seasonal landscape below. The flat stiles and rails of this screen are marbled.

Once pictures were physically separate from their architectural setting, frames were essential, and as early as the seventeenth century framing became a distinct craft. In *A Treatise of Japaning* (1688) Stalker and Parker describe a type of frame which was considered suitable for much amateur work: 'Your Frames for glass-painting [by which the authors meant transfer prints on glass] are usually made of stained Pear-tree, with narrow mouldings for little pieces, which increases in breadth, as the size of your picture does in largeness . . .'[29] These pear-tree frames were stained black in imitation of ebony, with a narrow carved and gilded front edge adjacent to the picture surface. Today frames of this type are loosely known as 'Hogarths', and the sensible recommendation that their width should be related to the size of the picture is often disregarded.

In the eighteenth century variations on these simulated ebony frames were made to a scale that was suitable for portraits with a 'sight measurement' 24 ins by 30 ins or larger. Because of their relative simplicity and cheapness many pictures would have been framed in this way. Where possible a gilded 'slip' was reserved for that part of the frame which was adjacent to the picture surface. A painted slip would compete with the picture itself; gold, or for that matter silver, was more neutral. This gilded slip was invariably carved, and between it and the main body of the frame a flat strip was covered with sand that was gilded. Such disruption of the surface by carving and 'sanding' subdued the gilding (be it oil or water gilding) so that it would not detract from the picture.

In the first half of the nineteenth century a simple wide frame of triangular section became popular. The flat area sloping to the picture surface was either painted to simulate bird's-eye maple, rosewood or mahogany, or veneered with these woods. Examples of frames with simulated veneers are now more rare than those with actual veneers. Frames of this type were usually fitted with a simple uncarved gilded slip. In the later nineteenth century frames with an 'S' section and a 'German gold' slip (i.e. an imitation gold applied by means of hot rollers) were almost invariably veneered in bird's-eye maple. The widespread alternative was the dreary 'compo' frame which bore accretions of decoration cast in 'composition' (a type of gesso) in imitation of carving. Another favourite of the second half of the nineteenth century was the 'Oxford' frame, which Brodie and Middleton's *Practical Carver and Gilder's Guide* (c. 1880) described as 'suitable for sacred subjects . . . but [also] for portraits, and many other pictures [which] look well in them.'

Much amateur work was constructed out of shells, rolled paper, seeds and such materials and, being in relief, depended upon a 'shadow box' for its existence and its survival. Accordingly, these shadow boxes should be seen not as adjuncts but as an integral part of the total object. It is known that in America vernacular painters such as Edward Hicks made their own frames. In Britain, where the trade of carver and gilder was represented in practically every provincial town of any consequence (as is confirmed by the trade directories), it is likely that most naive painters, both professional and amateur, turned to these craftsmen to make their frames for them. Naive paintings by professional artists were usually sold framed. This is confirmed by the description of the 'limner' in *The Vicar of Wakefield* and by the gallery of naive pictures to be seen on the extreme left
42 of the view of *All Saints Church, Northampton*.

Exhibitions of naive art

In the spring of 1762 William Hogarth, together with Bonnell Thornton, organized an exhibition of a fictitious 'Society of Sign Painters'. The artists of the day no doubt saw this show as a satire on the exhibition organized by the Society of Arts in the Strand, but those with the wit to see with Hogarth's eye may have viewed the enterprise in a more serious light. In general it was condemned by reviewers as 'an insult to understanding' but they betray some uncertainty as to the intention of the exhibition by adding '. . . to raise [an] innocent Laugh in others seems to have been his chief Aim in the present Spectacle . . .'[30] Whatever the motives and whatever the effect that this experiment had upon eighteenth-century sensibilities it can now be seen as the first exhibition of a category of work not easily defined but today known unsatisfactorily as naive art.

Hogarth's intentions may have been mixed, but a clue is to be found in the following phrase from Horace (*Ars Poetica*) which was displayed prominently in the exhibition: *Spectatum admissi risum teneatis*; which may be translated, 'You who are let in to look restrain your laughter.' In addition to the signs the exhibition included

... a most magnificent Collection of Portraits, Landscapes, Fancy Pieces, Flower Pieces, History Pieces, Night Pieces, Sea Pieces, Sculpture Pieces, &c. &c. designed by the ablest Masters, and executed by the best Hands in these kingdoms ...[31]

Although isolated artists such as John Kay exhibited in group exhibitions where the standards may be described as 'various',[32] no further exhibitions such as Hogarth's of 1762 seem to have taken place until the Whitney Studio Club of New York City (now the Whitney Museum of American Art) organized an exhibition of American naive art in 1924. In Europe an awareness of the importance of naive painting emerged in France as a result of the interest that the work of Henri Rousseau (1844–1910) inspired. Even so, admiration for the *douanier* was tinged with derision. The famous dinner of 1908 held in 'honour' of Rousseau delighted Picasso's friends (among them Braque, Laurencin, Apollinaire and Gertrude Stein) 'who were fond of making fun of the poor old customs man.'[33]

In England, too, the enthusiasm for naive art was first developed by practising artists rather than art historians or critics (with the notable exception of H. S. Ede). One day in August 1928 Ben Nicholson and Christopher Wood were walking through St Ives when they passed an open door through which they saw 'some paintings of ships and houses on odd pieces of paper and cardboard.'[34] At that moment Alfred Wallis was discovered and English naive art found its first twentieth-century disciples. Wallis himself would 'refer to other artists as real artists, saying that he was not a real artist.'[35] Because he was one of the first in this century to be discovered, much more is known about him than earlier artists of his kind. Even his semi-literate letters have been preserved. They do much to confirm the notion that such artists draw the important truths of the mind's eye rather than the details of observed fact:

what i do mosley is what use To Bee out of my own memery what we may never see again . . .

Despite the enthusiasm for the work of Alfred Wallis and the vast 'popular' following for naive painting in countries other than Britain, relatively little attention has been focused on it in England. The 1958 exhibition of *English Popular Art* at the Museum of English Rural Life at Reading organized by Enid Marx and Margaret Lambert, *The Primitives* shown at the Rutland Gallery, London in 1967, the comparative exhibition of *American and British Folk Art* shown in 1976 at the American Embassy, London, and the touring *Kalman Collection* must be seen as exceptions.

Portraits of the people

PHOTOGRAPHIC PORTRAITS by means of the daguerreotype became available in 1839. This coincided with the first publication of Charles Dickens's novel *Nicholas Nickleby*, in Chapter Three of which a jobbing portrait painter is described, one of a species whose future was doomed by the camera:

A miniature painter [Miss La Creevy] lived there, for there was a large gilt frame screwed upon the street-door, in which were displayed, upon a black velvet ground, two portraits of naval dress coats with faces looking out of them, and telescopes attached; one of a young gentleman in a very vermilion uniform, flourishing a sabre; and one of a literary character with a high forehead, a pen and ink, six books, and a curtain. There was, moreover, a touching representation of a young lady reading a manuscript in an unfathomable forest, and a charming whole length of a large-headed little boy, sitting on a stool with his legs foreshortened to the size of salt-spoons. Besides these works of art, there were a great many heads of old ladies and gentlemen smirking at each other out of blue and brown skies, and an elegantly-written card of terms with an embossed border.

Dickens's description graphically brings to mind countless examples of naive portraits. Perhaps these vernacular painters and their customers were uncertain about the accuracy of their portraits and felt a need to reaffirm by means of these 'props' the occupation and status of the sitters. Whatever the reason, these portraits now have a less particular and therefore more universal appeal than is often the case with someone else's ancestors.

The demand for portraiture was always very great, even in a frontier society. The American portrait painter, John Singleton Copley, lamented that only the desire to perpetuate features in 'likenesses' saved painting from extinction in the colonies.[1] These painters may have been in demand, but their social position was often low. Despite this prejudice, however, a number of British-born naive painters worked in America, among them Thomas Chambers (1808–66) and Robert Cowan (1762–1846).[2] Another was the youthful John Hazlitt who worked in America as a portrait and miniature painter (to become a fully-fledged academic in his maturity). John and his better known brother, the essayist William Hazlitt, lived in New York and Massachusetts with their parents and sister Margaret from 1783 until 1787 when the whole family returned to Britain.[3]

The social status of these artists in Britain seems to have varied enormously. Hazlitt was the son of a clergyman and so was John Collier, better known as a writer by his pseudonym, Tim Bobbin. Collier is credited with having 'attempted some heads in profile with decent success', but as his patron Richard Townley went on to state in his biographical pamphlet,[4] portraiture 'did not hit his humour, for I have heard him say, when urged to go on in that line, that drawing heads and faces was as dry and insipid as leading a life without frolic and fun, unless he was allowed to *steal in* some leers of comic humour, or give a good dash of the caricature.' Collier's occupation as a schoolmaster was in contrast to most non-academic painters who derived a livelihood from the craft of painting. Among these was George Evans, referred to by Edward Edwards as 'a house painter, but frequently painted portraits . . . much cannot be said of his powers as an artist, nor will his portraits be much in request with posterity.'[5]

In the early nineteenth century drawing, together with music and dancing, came to be known collectively as 'accomplishments' suitable for young ladies: 'The chief object in the attainment of what are called *accomplishments*, ought to be to soften and refine the manners, and to add to the innocent and elegant enjoyments of human life.'[6] Among the books

5, 6

30

that were written to cater for this market were *An Introduction to Perspective ... Drawing and Painting ... Properly Adapted for the Instruction of Females* by Charles Hayter (1816), and *The Miniature Painter's Manual Containing Progressive Lessons on the Art of Drawing and Painting Likenesses from Life* by Nathaniel Whittock (1844). In Chapter 2 of his book Whittock makes the shrewd observation that 'the learner will find it advisable to draw the profile of the face, selecting a sitter with a strongly marked angular countenance ... Elderly persons are much more easily painted than young ones; their features are more prominent, and the lines more defined ...'

Profile portraits and silhouettes were of course made by both professionals and amateurs, and both used various devices where, by means of shadows cast on paper or the camera obscura, the profile could be

22–25   rendered with near-photographic accuracy. The series of late eighteenth-century profile portraits illustrated on page 46 have a truth to nature that suggests that they were probably drawn with the aid of a 'physiognotrace' which accounts for the artist's unflattering veracity in the profiles. In contrast, details within the silhouette reveal the artist's limited conventional ability in the cramped drawing of the hands. This series of portraits, which apparently shows several generations of one family, appears to be the work of a professional artist. Perrenon's book published in London in 1780, *The Physiognomical Cabinet, A Detailed Treatise on Silhouettes, Their Drawing, Reduction, Ornamentation and Reproduction*, was designed for use by amateurs and lays great stress on the equipment they would need.

In the second half of the nineteenth century, when education for the masses became an important issue, a new type of naive painter appeared who had had some art, as opposed to craft, training. Typical of these was Joseph Sheppard (1834–1928), a farmer's son born near Weston-super-Mare. In 1866 Sheppard (a student of James A. Davis) was awarded a prize in Weston-super-Mare for a watercolour drawing of a group of apples, and this was followed on 24 April 1867 by a 'Certificate from the Council of Education for success in Freehand or Model Drawing'. Most surviving examples of Sheppard's work (mainly landscapes and portraits)

28   date from this period. His portrait of Miss Bisdee of Grove House, Worle, who was the daughter of a member of the local gentry, is perhaps his finest work.[7]

There can be little doubt that it is an imperative of human nature to possess likenesses of those who are nearest and dearest. This characteristic is probably most pronounced in time of war. A number of poignant watercolour drawings of humble private soldiers survive which seem to have been made by professionals and amateurs as keepsakes for the friends and families of soldiers serving overseas. A particularly attractive example is the mid nineteenth-century portrait of *Joseph Pestell, of Her Majesty's 21st Regiment, and his family*. The intention of these pictures is underlined by the verse that appears beneath one such drawing:

2, 3

4

> In many a hardship have I been
>   With many a thousand more;
> But we will hope soon to return
>   To our dear native shore . . .
> O! grant ye Powers that rule above
>   Our son may grow in grace;
> And may he still protected be
>   In every dangerous place . . .
> Dear AUNT accept this trifling Gift
>   This token of good will;
> For though we are now far from you
>   Yet we shall love you still.[8]

The word 'aunt' has here clearly been added in a different hand in the space provided for the purpose.

These pictures are not so much portraits as representations of soldiers in appropriate uniforms made in the same spirit as a medieval effigy of a knight in an English parish church. Photography removed the necessity for such pictures and drained the life blood from a vernacular art that had once held great force by virtue of the popular level at which it was consumed.

1 *Admiral Lord Exmouth*, a watercolour portrait >
of the great naval hero of the Napoleonic wars,
Edward Pellew (1757–1833), who became the
first Viscount Exmouth in 1814.

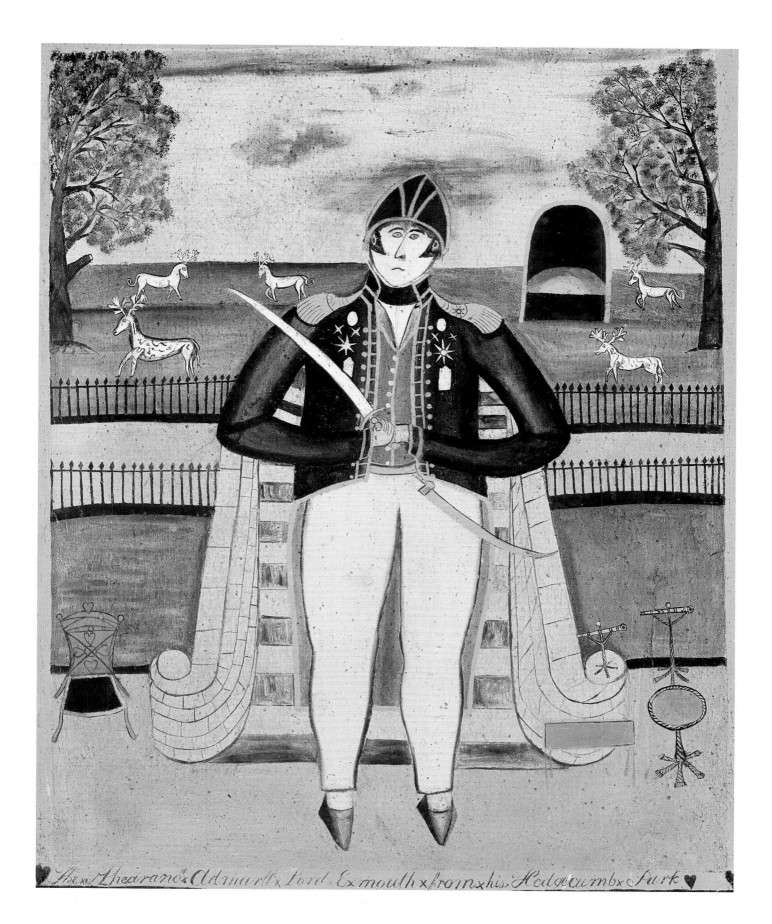

The Apearance Admaralt Lord Exmouth from his Hedgcumb Park

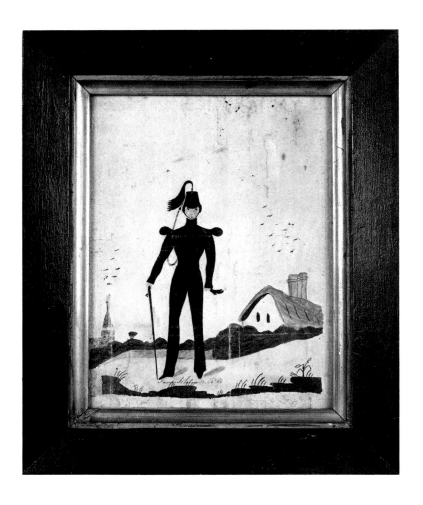

4 *Joseph Pestell, Wife and Child, 1844, of Her* > *Majesty's 21st Regiment, Or Royal North British Fusiliers*, watercolour with sequins. Such pictures were often painted for private soldiers about to be posted abroad and separated from their families.

2,3 Watercolour portraits of soldiers, perhaps intended as keepsakes: above, *James Johnson RB* (Rifle Brigade), mid nineteenth century, with an embossed decorative edge on the paper of the border – a feature it shares with two similar 'military portrait' watercolours in the National Army Museum; right, *Charles Norton IX Regt, c.* 1840–45.

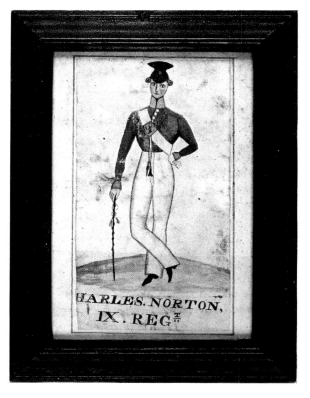

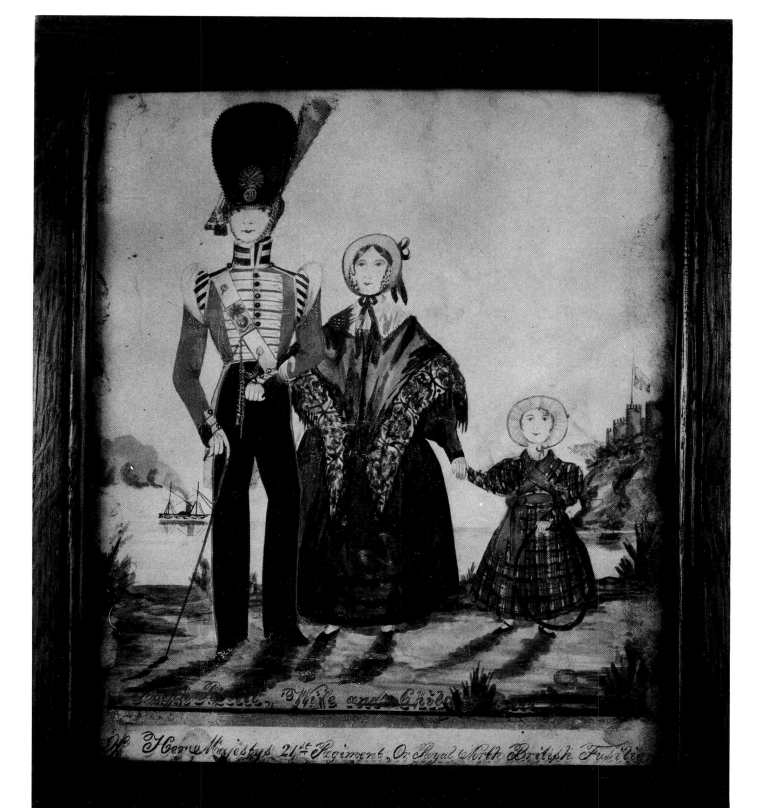

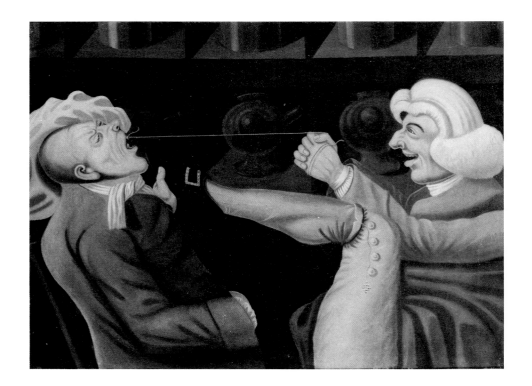

7 *Gretna Green Ceremony*, > nineteenth-century, oil on board. At the famous smithy on the Scottish border a pious blacksmith is shown uniting the eloping couple.

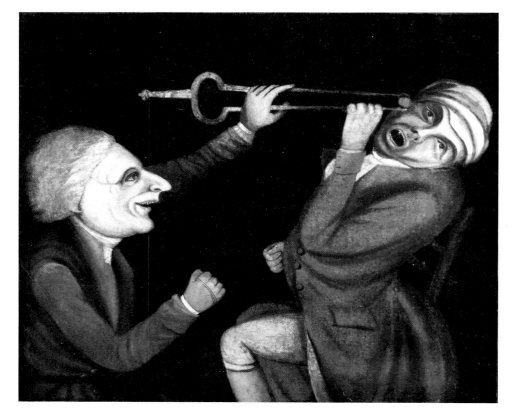

5,6 Popular dentistry: two oil paintings by John Collier (1708–86), alias Tim Bobbin, related to engravings for his *Human Passions Delineated* (1772–3). Collier's work was sought by 'merchants in Liverpool who sent them upon speculation into the West Indies and America', though the artist admitted to only liking portrait work if he was 'allowed to steal in some leers of comic humour'.

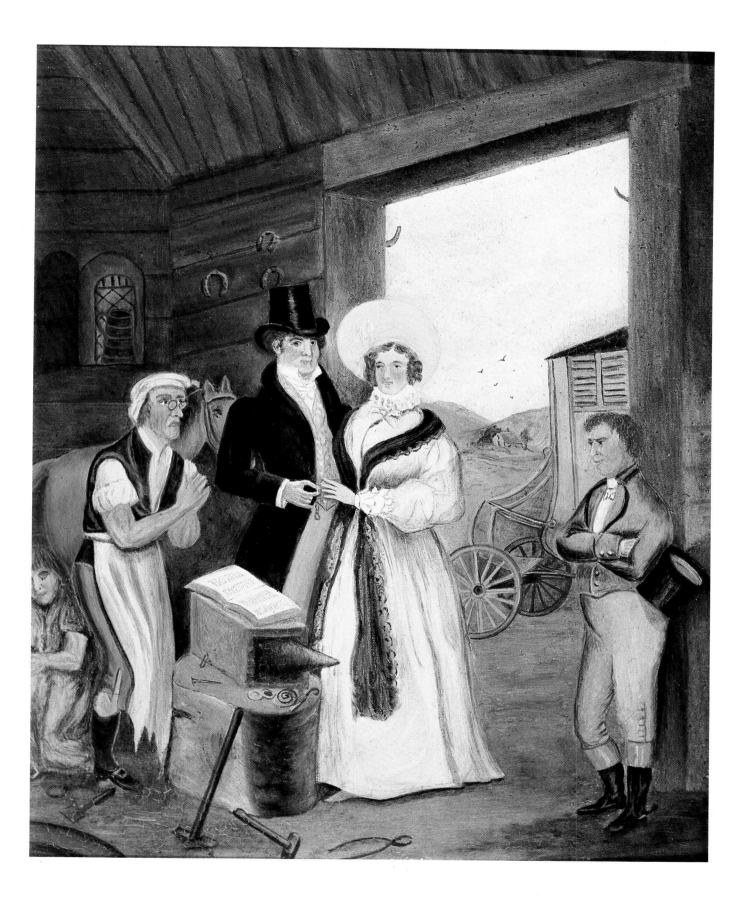

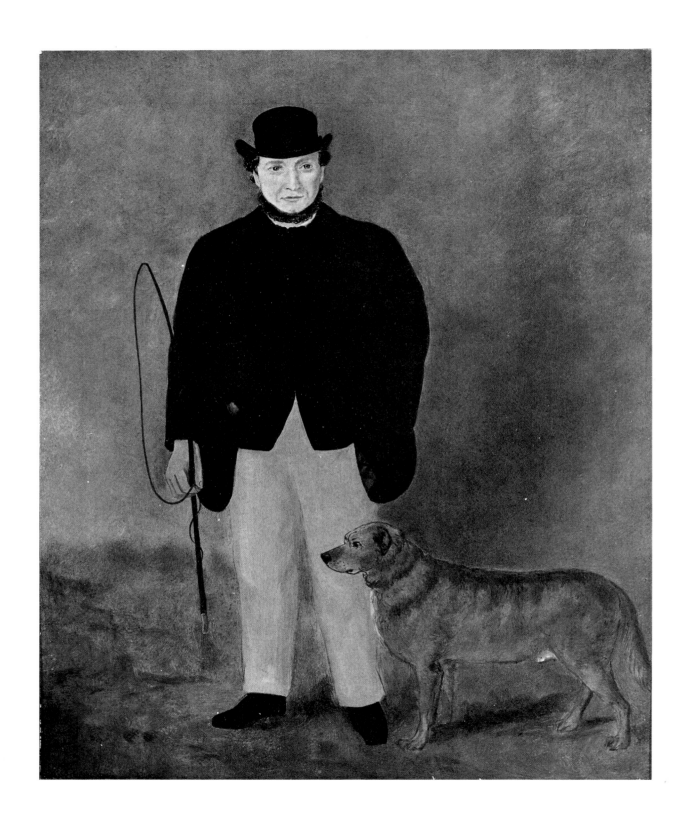

8 *The Drover*, by T. G. Audlay, *c.* 1860, a portrait in oils of a prosperous member of
the artisan class, shown with the symbols of his trade, a dog and a whip.

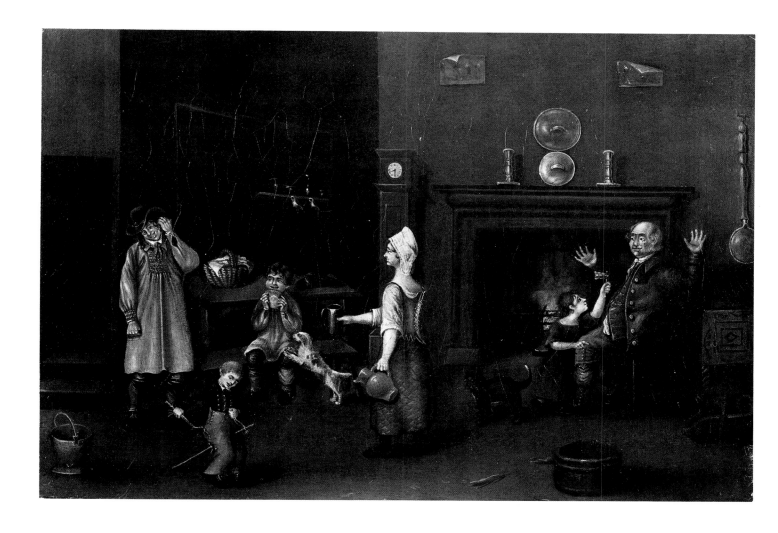

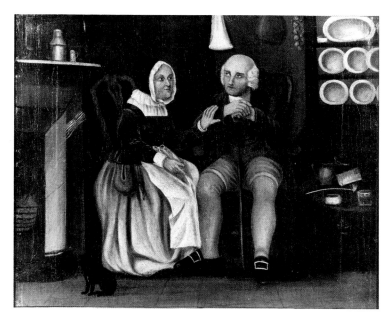

9,10 Two interiors: above, *The Happy Family*, an early nineteenth-century oil painting showing the kind of details – in the smock and the quilted skirt – that enables naive art to widen our knowledge of the period; left, *The Elderly Couple*, late eighteenth-century oil on panel.

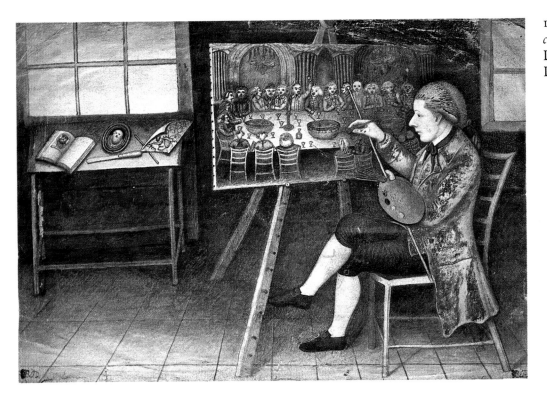

13 Opposite, *The Family Group,* c. 1880, an oil painting from Liverpool, perhaps of a rising Lancashire merchant and family.

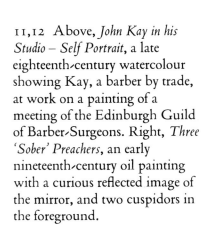

11,12 Above, *John Kay in his Studio – Self Portrait,* a late eighteenth-century watercolour showing Kay, a barber by trade, at work on a painting of a meeting of the Edinburgh Guild of Barber-Surgeons. Right, *Three 'Sober' Preachers,* an early nineteenth-century oil painting with a curious reflected image of the mirror, and two cuspidors in the foreground.

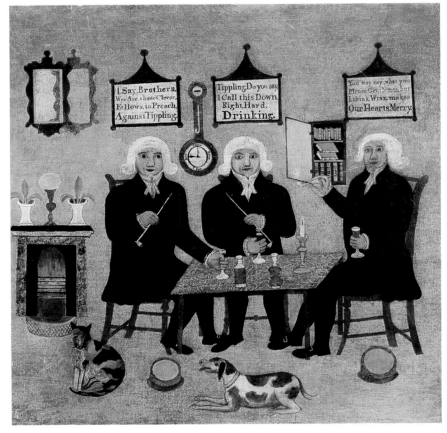

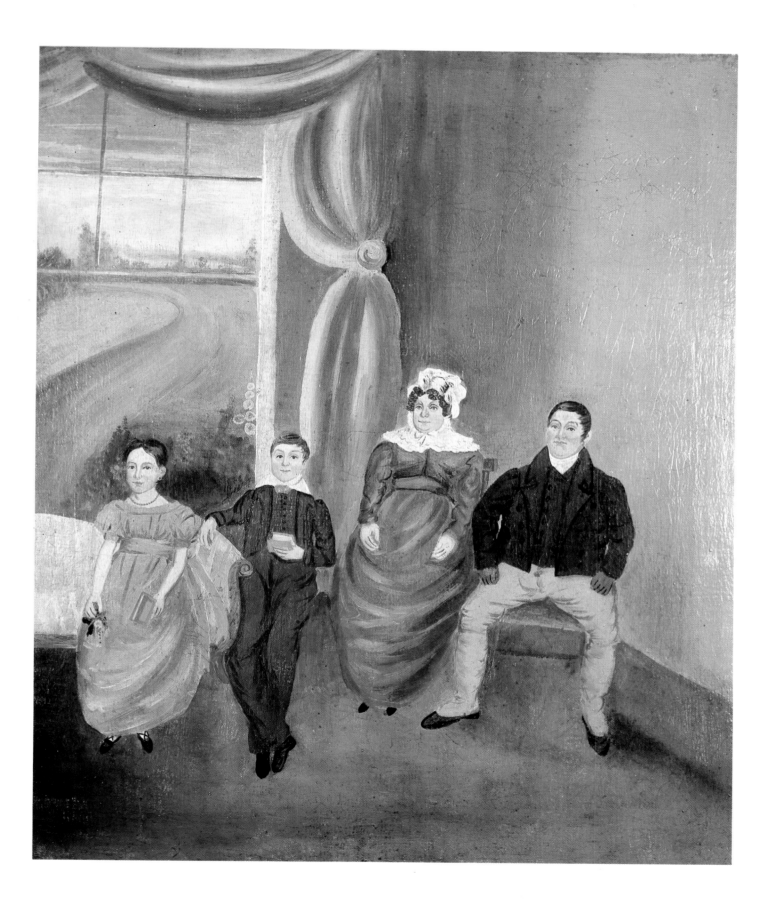

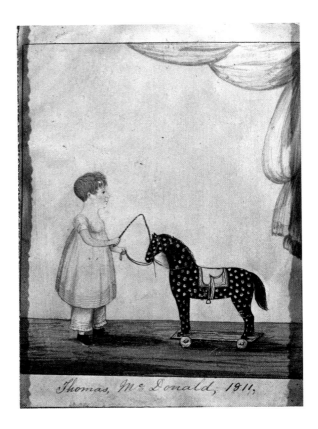

Thomas, McDonald, 1811,

14,15 Left, *Thomas McDonald*, 1811, watercolour on paper. Below, *The Ladies' Boarding School*, c. 1780–1800, ink and watercolour on paper. This picture may well have been painted by one of the elegant young ladies which it portrays.

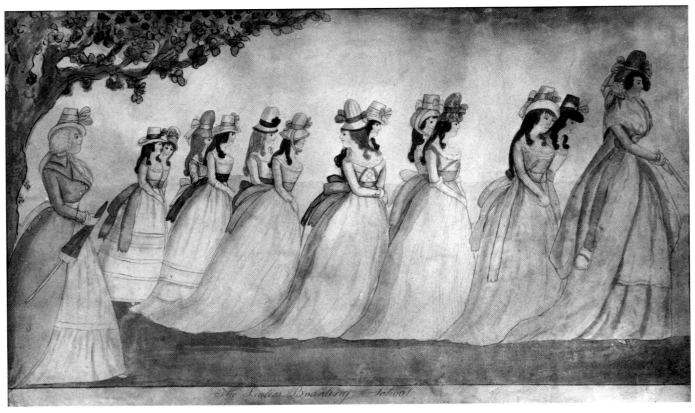

The Ladies Boarding School

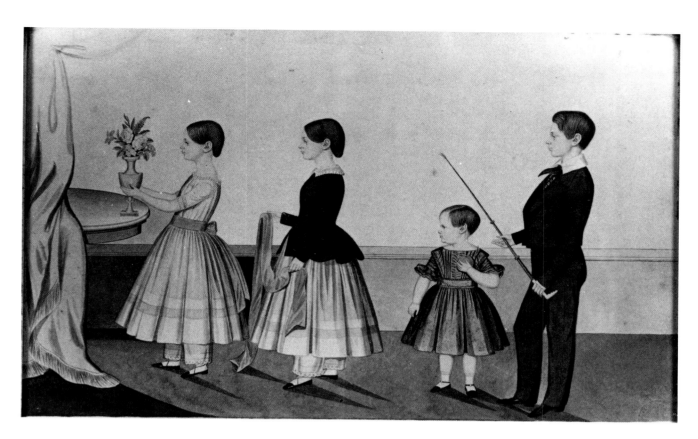

16,17 Above, *Profile Portrait of Four Children*, a mid nineteenth-century watercolour. The painter's attempt to suggest a source of light by means of attractively geometric shadows is rarely found in naive art. Right, in *Profile Portrait of a Fat Boy*, the asymmetric arrangement of the figure and chaise longue is ingeniously 'centred' with the patterned floor.

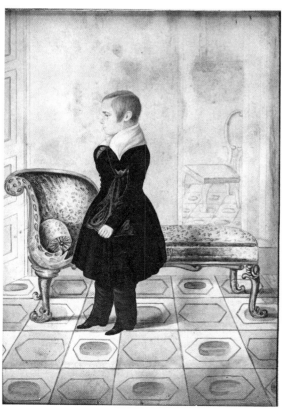

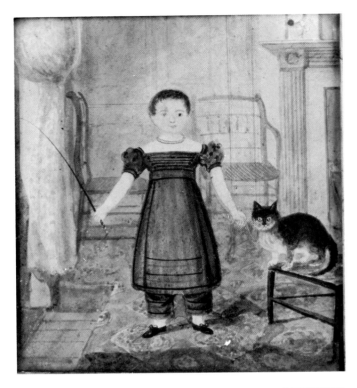

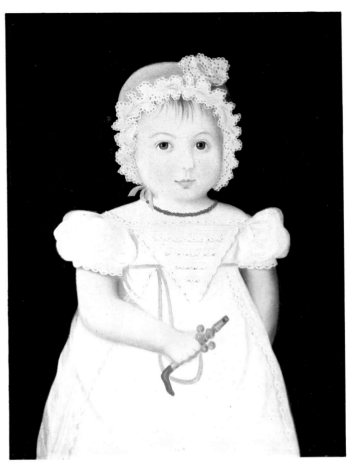

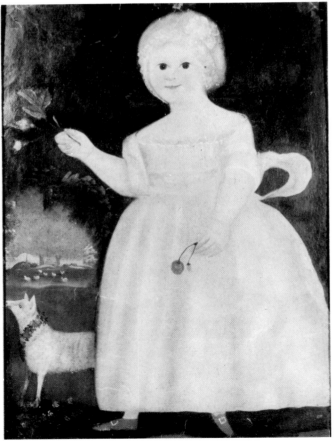

18,19 Above left, *A Child with a Cat*, early
nineteenth-century watercolour, provides
meticulous and informative background details
of architecture and furnishings. Left, *A Child
with a Lamb*, oil on panel, suggests religious
overtones with the garlanded lamb and the
church in the background.

20,21 Opposite, *Alfred Openshaw, Age One
Year*, by R. Hunt, 1846, oil on canvas. The
coral necklace indicates a superstition inherited
from the Romans that coral warded off evil from
children. In *A Child with a Coral*, above, the
same notion recurs in the silver and coral rattle.

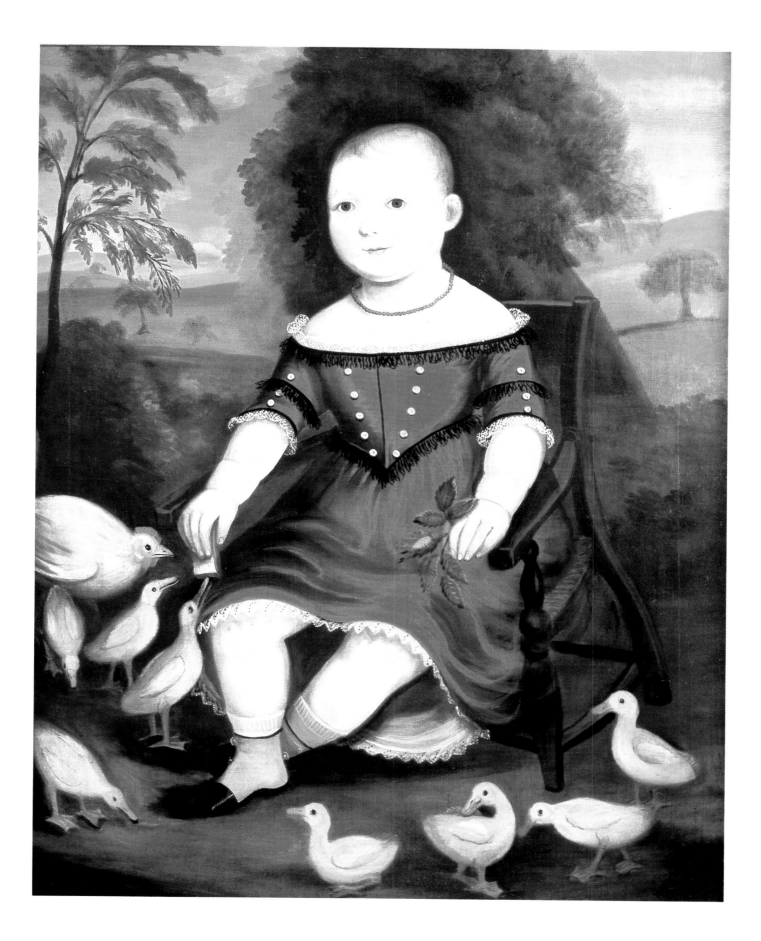

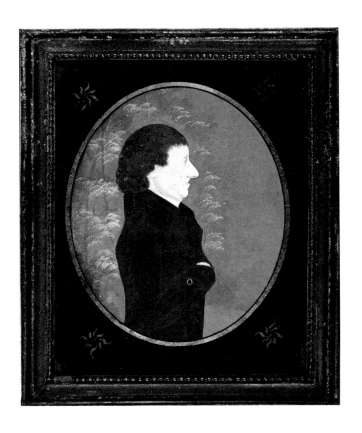
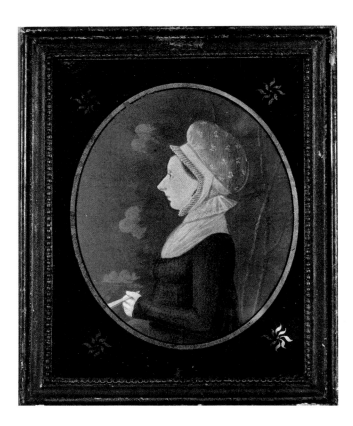
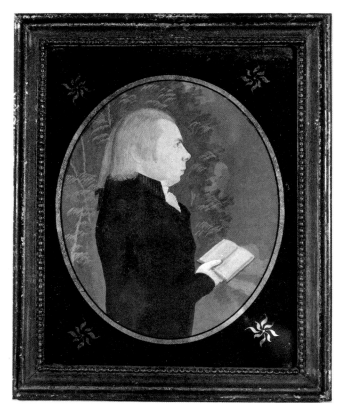
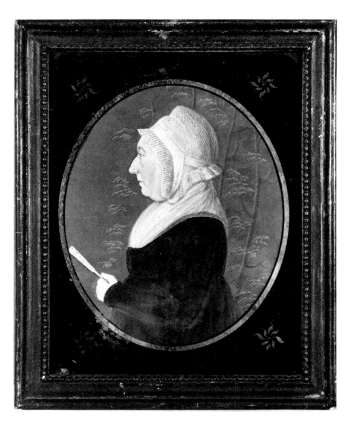

22,23,24,25 Opposite, a set of portraits, *c.* 1800, gouache on paper, with original framing and glazing. The glass has been gilded and given a coat of Brunswick black to provide the oval 'window mounts'. Through mechanical devices like the physiognotrace, great accuracy could be achieved in the silhouette outlines of the portraits, but within the outline the drawing was less conventionally accurate.

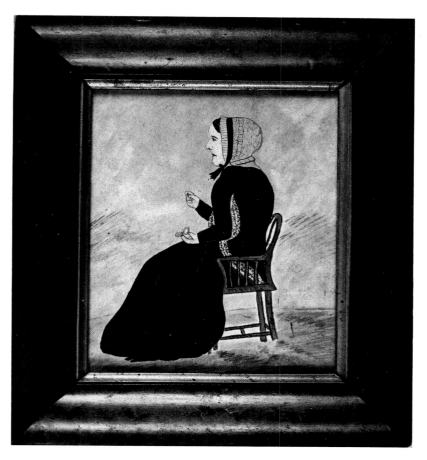

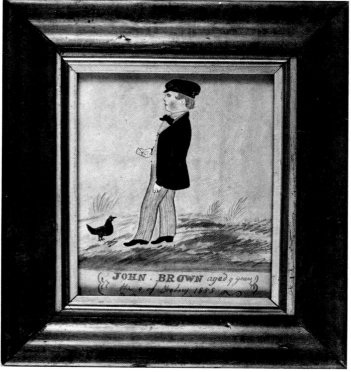

26,27 Left, *John Brown aged 9 Years, the 9 of Febary 1855*, watercolour in contemporary maple frame. Above, *Profile of an Old Lady Taking Snuff*, in the same series, may depict John Brown's grandmother.

28 Overleaf, *Portrait of Miss Bisdee*, by Joseph Sheppard (1834–1928), *c.* 1866–70, oil on canvas. Until recent restoration, the tree on the left bore a sign reading 'Beware of Man Traps'. Miss Bisdee, of Grove House, Worle, married and went to Australia, where she had sixteen children.

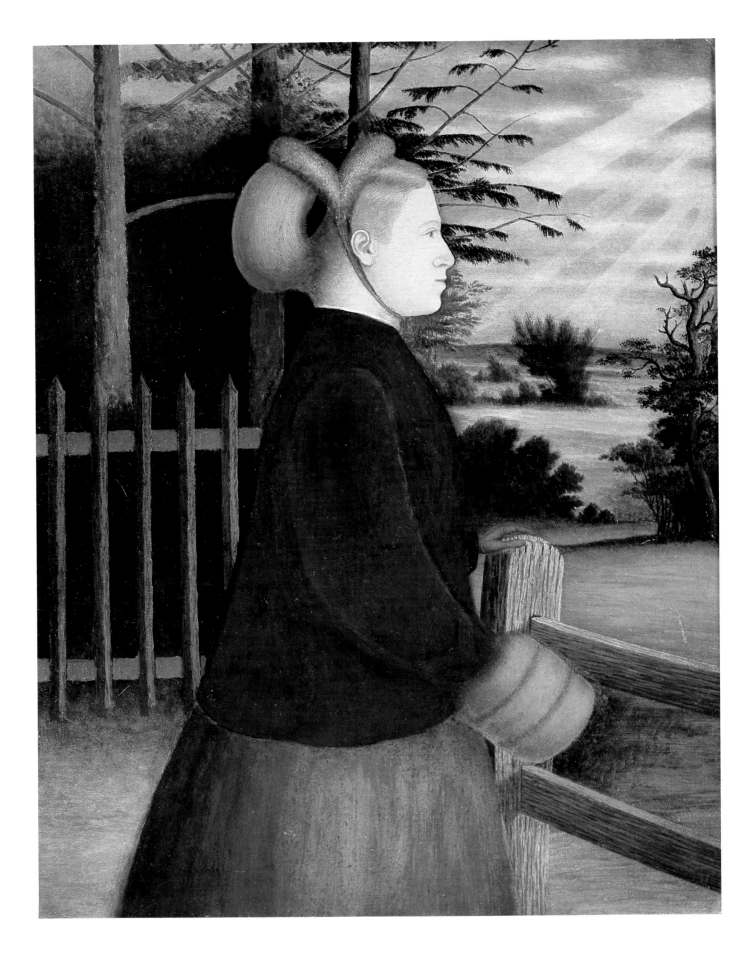

Town life

WHEN IN THE SECOND HALF of the eighteenth century the Satanic mills first appeared in England's green and pleasant land they were, as Blake's imagery suggests and Joseph Wright's paintings show, but isolated phenomena by day which assumed their demonic threat by night. In the first half of the nineteenth century the increase in urbanization was particularly marked in the Midlands where '. . . the traveller passed rapidly from one phase of English Life to another; after looking down on a village dingy with coal-dust, noisy with shaking looms, he might skirt a parish all of fields, high hedges, and deep rutted lanes . . . a rural region where the neighbourhood of the town was only felt in the advantages of a near market for corn, cheese, and hay . . .'[1] Rural areas like Failsworth (see p. 86) would be swallowed up by Manchester, and New Brentford, once a busy market town in Middlesex, would be engulfed by Greater London.

68

33

46   Until the Industrial Revolution urban skylines were clearly punctuated by their churches in towns and by their cathedrals in cities. In the industrialized towns of Victorian England a new order was visible, broken by factory chimneys, a feature most noticeable in the textile centres of East Lancashire and the West Riding of Yorkshire (which in our own century were to be immortalized by L. S. Lowry). Unfortunately nineteenth-century photographs and prints of these bustling towns are rare

except when their purpose was to record some civic event or royal visit.[2] In the eighteenth century Hogarth was among the few artists who looked at the harsher realities of town life, and even in the nineteenth century the French engraver Gustave Doré was an exception in recognizing the drama of London's squalor. In general it was not until the close of the nineteenth century that painters began to exploit these scenes of industrial buildings with their murky skies. A number of paintings show how naive artists could and did express these new spectacles in an idiom without precedent resulting from a subject without antecedents.

38,39

Despite the revolutionary change that the nineteenth century wrought on the face of England some cities and towns are still recognizable by the landscape which underlies a vastly changed skyline. An obvious example of this is the *View of Scarborough* but the same applies to the painting of the *Broad Quay, Bristol* by an unidentified artist in the first half of the eighteenth century. This view would have been familiar to late seventeenth-century travellers down to details such as the transport that it illustrates. Writing of Bristol in 1699 Celia Fiennes mentions '. . . their using sleds to carry all things about . . .'[3]

120

43

In towns, of course, change and redevelopment destroyed more than it preserved, but fortunately because so many naive paintings were conceived as documents of record, the topographical views may be accepted with some confidence. On occasion a striking survival of a building may be established by comparison with one of these paintings, such as *The Eagle Tavern, Fulham.*

34,34a

Out of recognition of the necessity for improved roads grew the development of new methods of transport, a feature which many of these paintings reflect. Naturally they show the mail coach, the pre-eminent form of transport before the coming of the railways. Indeed such pictures may well have been commissioned by the inn keeper outside whose hostelry these vehicles are invariably painted. It is just possible that one artist may have painted the sign, repeated it on the coach panel and painted pictures of the inns and the coach, each of which bore examples of his work.[4] Other vehicles shown include the covered carrier's wagon painted in the traditional colours of red wheels and blue body as for farm carts. The same picture includes an interesting tradesman's delivery vehicle, a covered

80, 87

33

wheelbarrow. These were presumably used to transport dry goods for short distances. A print by Bowles and Carver shows a covered wheelbarrow for 'Hot Spice Gingerbread'.[5]

Ford Madox Brown's *Work* of 1852–65 illustrates an apparent harmony of the classes and a cleanliness of the air which would not have satisfied the naive urban artist of his time, and the mid nineteenth-century paintings of these artists, for all their simplicity, reveal the bleak truths of urban life in their total mood. Not for nothing does drink provide an ever-present theme in many of these pictures – for example 'Tetley's Fine 37, 38 Ales', 'Darley's Fine Ales' and 'W. Morrell, Licensed Dealer in Wines, Foreign & British Spirits, Beer, Porter & Tobacco'.

The naive artist may sometimes have permitted compositions to arrive by accident rather than intention, or to have failed to handle tonal qualities with conventional tonal recession, but these artists nearly always had a good eye for detail which is perhaps most noticeable in urban subjects. They in fact obeyed William Blake's dictum that 'to Generalize is to be an Idiot. To Particularize is the Alone Distinction of Merit.'[6]

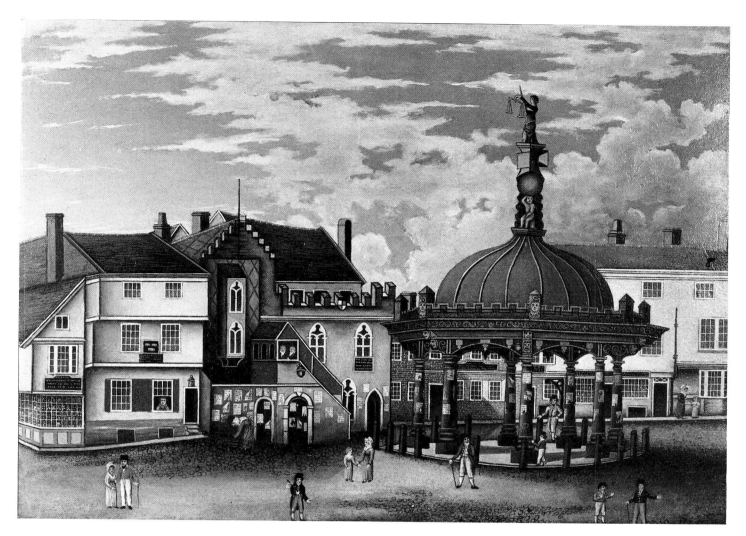

29 *The Market Cross*, Ipswich, oil on board, painted shortly before its demolition in 1812. The same 'improvements' swept away the front of the Old Town Hall (here shown plastered with public notices), removing the flight of stairs 'clumsy, steep and dangerous' (G. R. Clarke, *History of Ipswich*, 1830) leading to the upper chambers. The original cross was erected in 1520, and the Town Hall was converted from one of the town's most ancient churches.

30 Below, *Model Butcher's Shop*, 1875–90,
carved wood, painted, in its original cross-
boarded mahogany shadow box. Possibly used
for instruction, these models of various carcasses
and cuts of meat were made with great care.
The Royal Arms (the sign of royal patronage) is
probably a military cap badge.

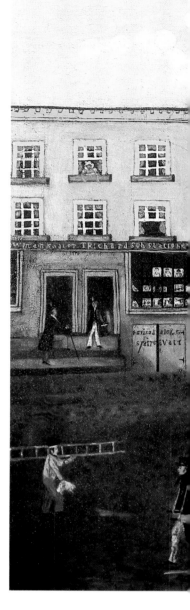

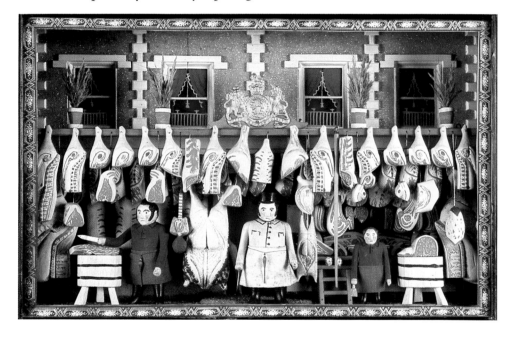

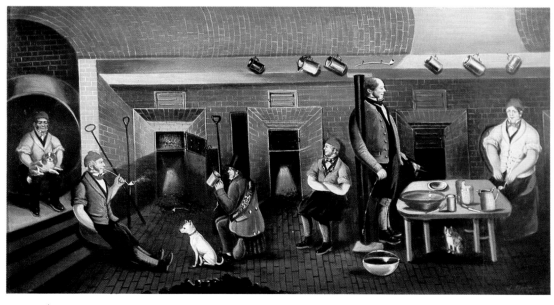

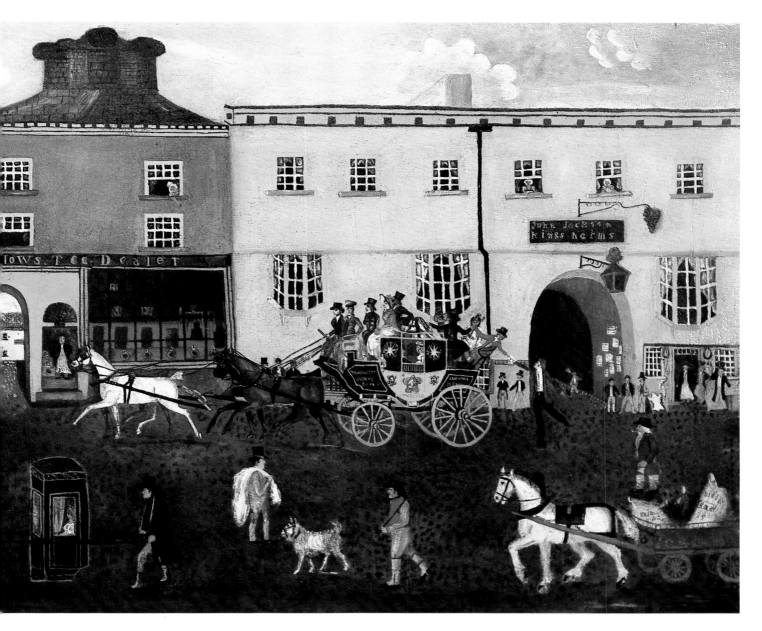

31 Above, *The Kings Arms, Manchester*,
*c.*1829–30, oil on canvas. The contemporary
Manchester *Directories* show that the Liverpool
coach ran from the Kings Arms (here spelt
'harms'), King Street, near Deansgate.

32 Opposite, *The Royal Rat Catcher*, by
J. Clark, early nineteenth-century oil on canvas,
showing that gentleman with pint pot, top hat,
and sash of office. Clark was from Hoxton,
London, and sometimes described himself as
'Animal Painter to the Queen'.

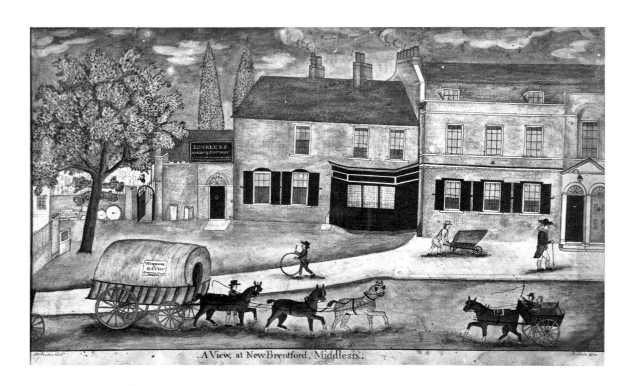

A View, at New Brentford, Middlesex.

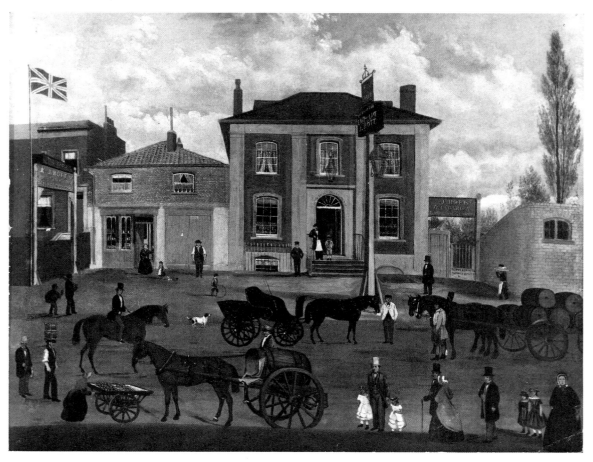

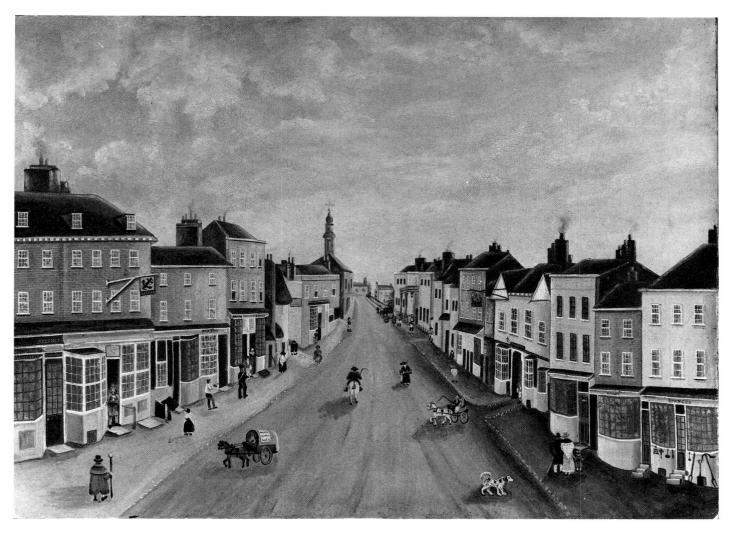

33 Opposite above, *A View, at New Brentford, Middlesex*, by H. Sexton, 1804, watercolour on paper, commemorating the former market town of Middlesex. The covered wheelbarrow is a tradesman's delivery vehicle, and the carrier's cart in the foreground is painted in the traditional colours of red for wheels and blue for body.

34,34a Opposite, *The Eagle*, or *Lady of the Lake Inn*, 1857, oil on canvas. Right, the premises survive, somewhat altered, in Fulham, London, still called *The Eagle*.

35 *The High Street, Staines*, an early nineteenth-century oil painting, showing a beadle with his staff, and a handsome display of ironmongers' tools, right foreground.

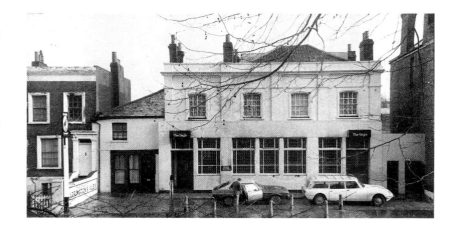

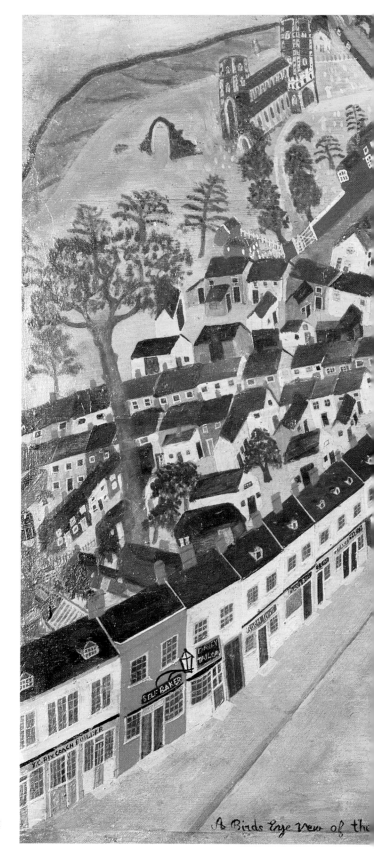

36 *A Bird's Eye View of Market Street,
Wymondham, c.* 1850, oil on canvas, with the
bird itself included in the picture. The ruined
abbey in the background was the subject of a
long feud between monks and townspeople,
settled when in 1249 the Pope granted the east
end to the monks and the west to the town.

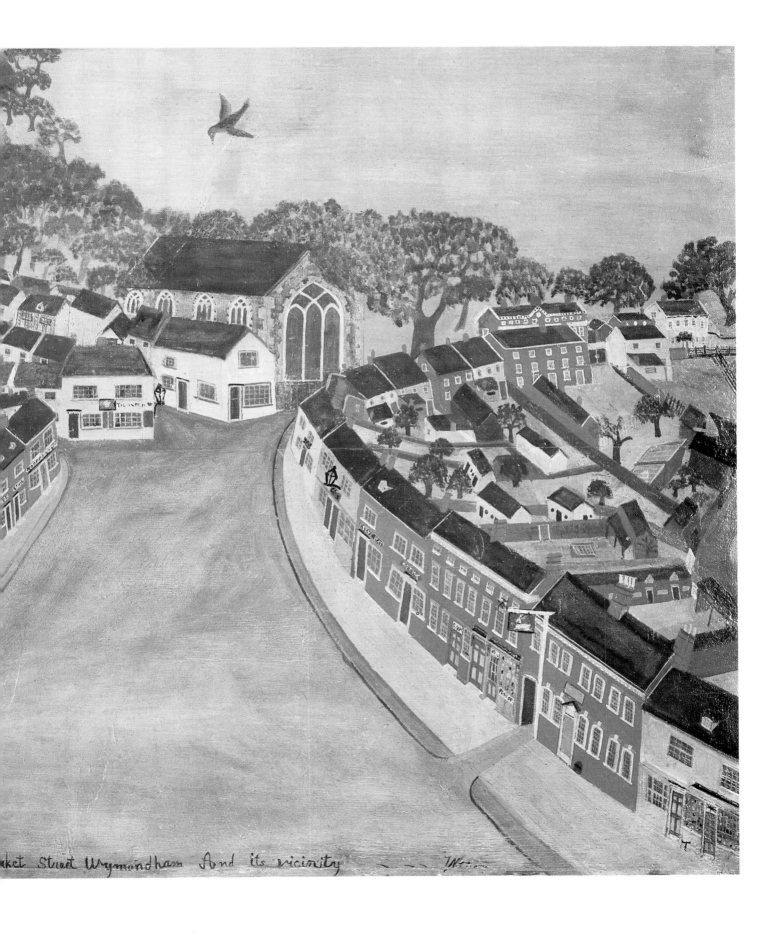

ket Street Wymondham And its vicinity ~ ~ Ufee

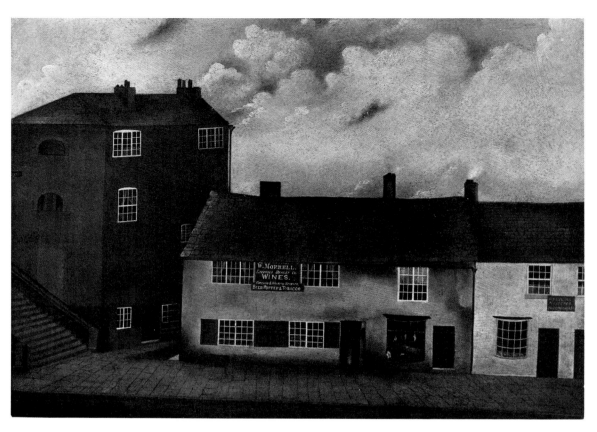

37 *Wakefield, Old Church Steps at the Entrance to Teal Street*, by C. H. Hepworth, 1852, oil on board. The sombre mood of this industrial townscape seems to anticipate the work of L. S. Lowry.

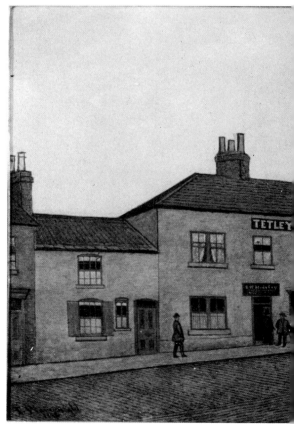

38 Right, *A Yorkshire Street Corner* (possibly Castleton), by T. Wainwright, 1892, oil on canvas. Tetley's breweries are based in Leeds.

39 Opposite above, *A. Marshall, Dyer and Scourer*, by Arthur Godwin, 1908, oil on canvas. The sign on the right reads 'Public Vaccination Station'. Vaccination became compulsory in 1853.

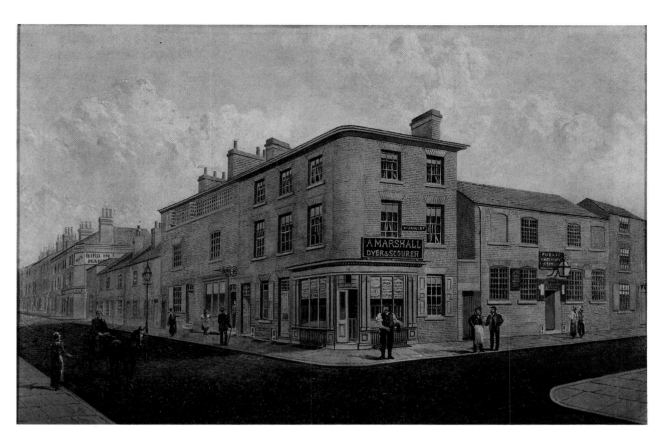

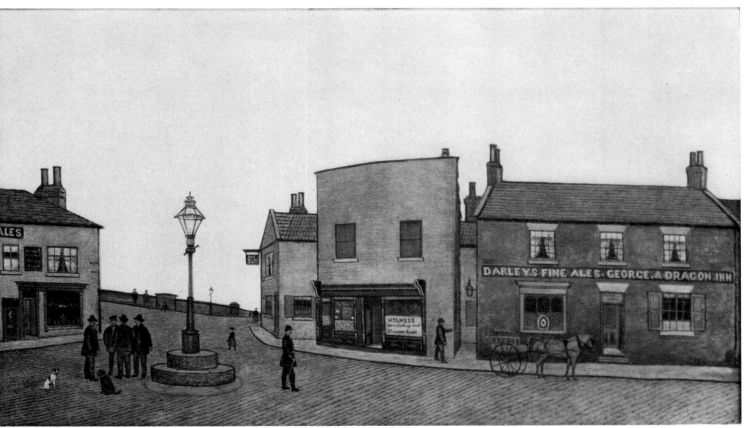

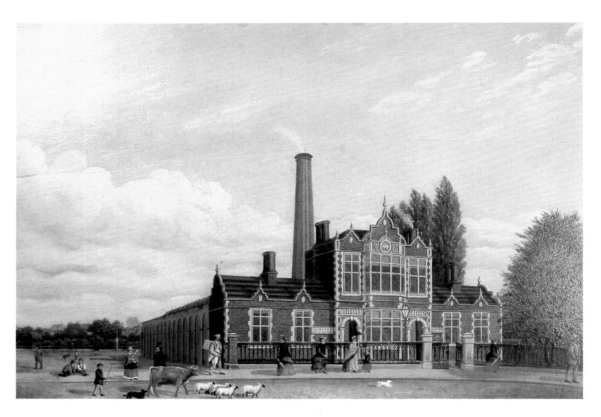

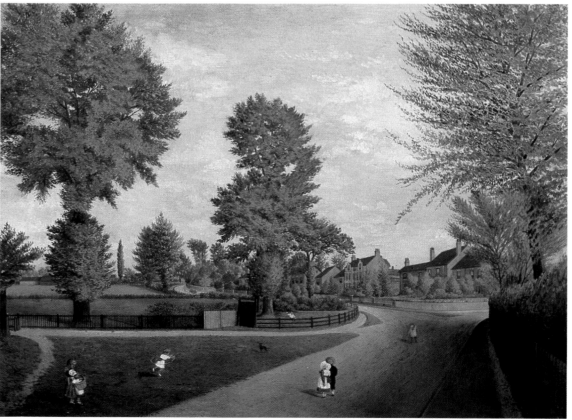

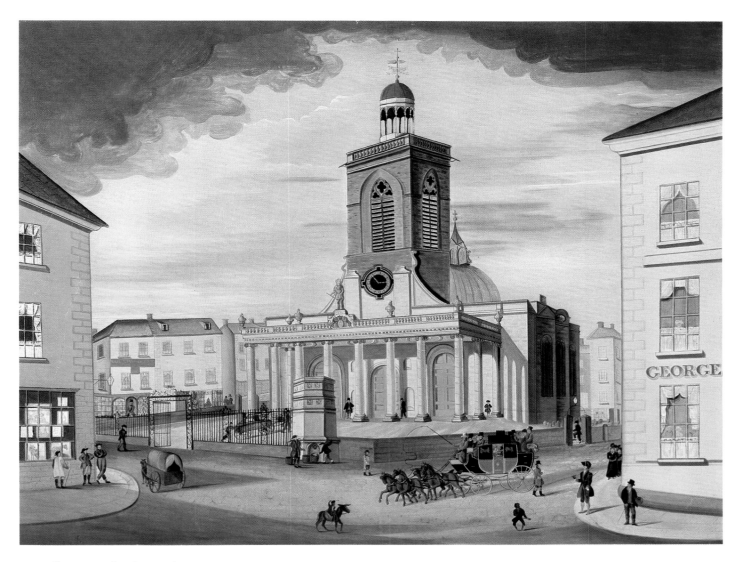

42 *All Saints Church, Northampton*, c. 1830–35,
oil on canvas. The artist may have been the
owner of the gallery showing naive paintings,
left, where the works on sale are ready framed.
In another, almost identical, version, the church
clock is a working watch mechanism, inset
from behind.

40,41 Opposite, Two views of nineteenth-
century Coventry: above, *The Public Baths*, by
W. E. Reeve, 1873; below, *The Park*, by
Herbert Rylance, c. 1885. Earlsdon library was
built on this site.

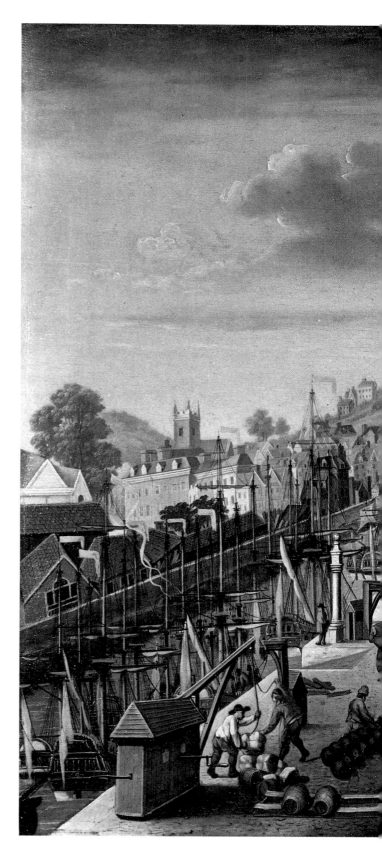

43 *Broad Quay, Bristol*, an early eighteenth-century oil painting of England's principal (with Liverpool) New World port. The use of sleds in Bristol, bottom right, was commented on in 1699 by Celia Fiennes in her journal.

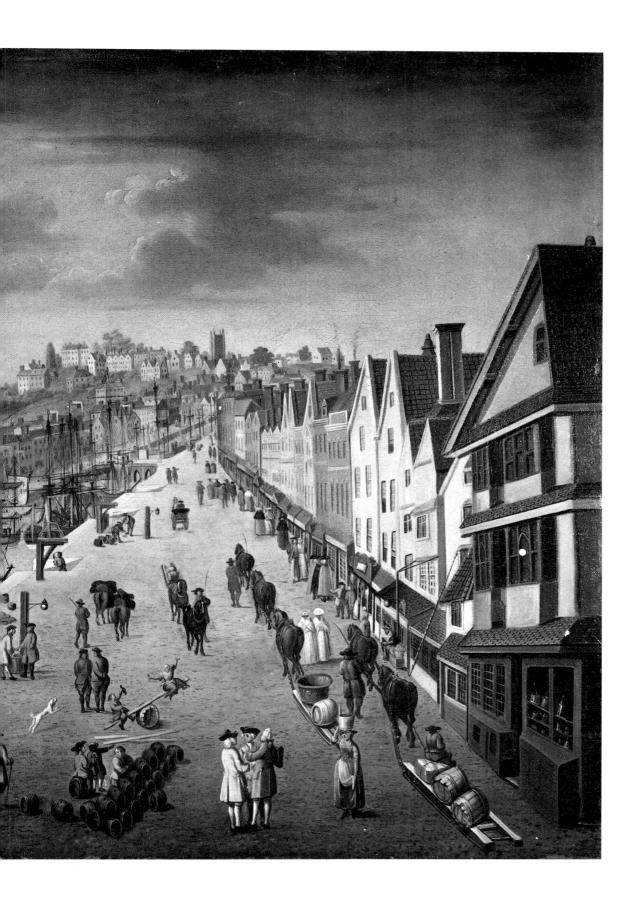

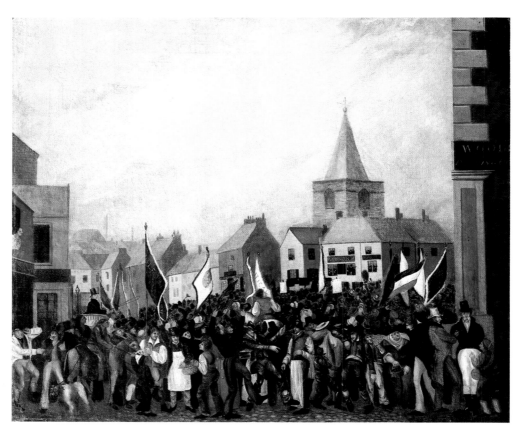

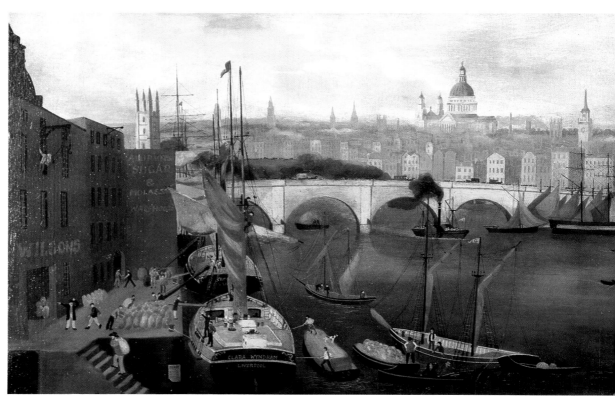

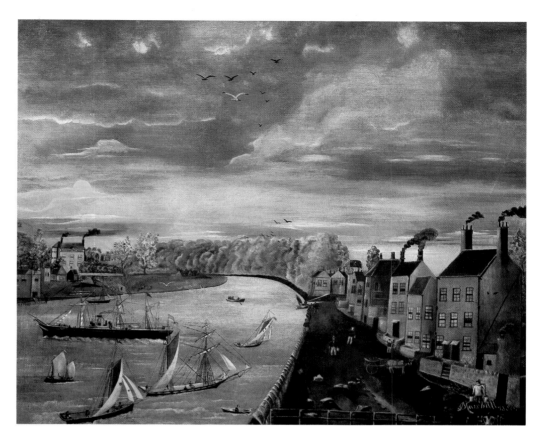

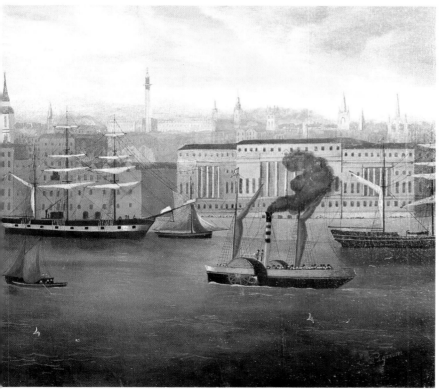

44 Opposite, *An Election Meeting, Blackburn Market Place, 1832*, oil on canvas. The year of the first Reform Act saw the election of three Liberal MPs by this Lancashire industrial town.

45 Above, *A View of Bristol*, by J. Marshall, 1880, oil on canvas. On the left is the Lamplighter's Arms inn, below which lies a steamship flying an American flag.

46 *A Riverside View of London*, c. 1840–50, oil on canvas. A Liverpool-registered boat, foreground, unloads a cargo (of sugar?) at Wilson's wharf.

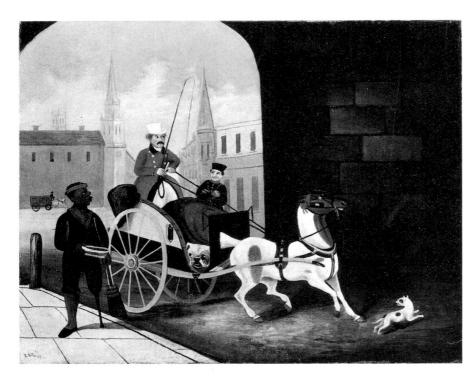

47 *The Black Street Sweeper*, by B. Sturr, *c.* 1850, oil on canvas.

48 Below, *Waiting outside Number 12*, *c.* 1850, oil on canvas. The artist has provided this modest house, unremarkable except for its external shutters, with an imposing sense of isolation, as though it were the only building in the street.

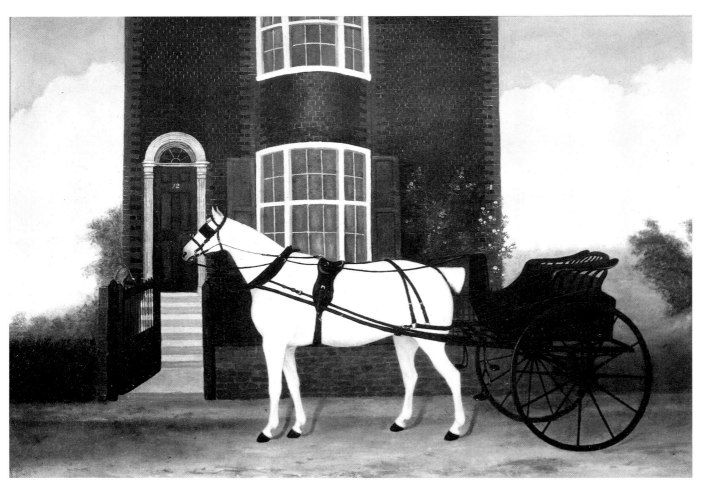

Sports and pastimes

'IN ORDER TO FORM a just estimation of the character of any particular people, it is absolutely necessary to investigate the Sports and Pastimes most generally prevalent among them.'[1] Strutt's magisterial statement is no doubt valid but it could be added that the representation of such activities by painters is an important indication of the relative worth given to leisure in relationship to art.

Aside from the work of anonymous artists, Francis Barlow (1626–1704) was the first native English artist to specialize in sporting and animal pictures, and through engravings his work proved to be a source of inspiration to vernacular artists into the early nineteenth century. Because the clients for much of this type of painting were obsessed by the subject matter they were often indifferent to the quality of the painting. It is probably for this reason that such subjects range from the sophistication of Stubbs to the inimitable charm of John Whitehead. Edward Edwards cites a certain Richard Roper as 'a painter of sporting pieces, race-horses, dogs and dead game. He lived sometime in Little St Martin's Lane, was an exhibitor at the room in Spring Garden in 1761 and the succeeding year, but did not long survive that period. His powers as an artist were not considerable, yet sufficient to satisfy the gentlemen of the turf and stable.'[2]

68

A painted screen clearly illustrates the range of subject matter painted by these 'inconsiderable' artists. The screen shows that the English country squire or farmer could lose money in a variety of interesting ways that are also referred to in a ballad called *New Market* in D'Urfrey's collection of songs quoted by Strutt:[3]

> Let cullies that lose at a race
> Go venture at hazard to win,
> Or he that is bubbl'd at dice
> Recover at cocking again;
> Let jades that are founder'd be bought,
> Let jockeys play crimp to make sport . . .
> . . . Another makes racing a trade,
> And dreams of his projects to come;
> And many a crimp match has made,
> By bubbing another man's groom.[4]

In the eighteenth century fox-hunting became more general than the earliest sports of stag-hunting and falconry, as is reflected by the number of paintings of these subjects. Racing, the 'Sport of Kings', was less often painted by out-and-out naive artists, though there are of course exceptions. Certainly there were many painters whose lack of training or talent places their work in an aesthetic limbo that may verge on the naive, despite the grandeur of some of their patrons. Some such artists received no professional training, among them James Seymour (1702–52), Thomas Butler (*fl.* 1750–55), David Morier (1705?–70) and the Sartorius family, Francis Sartorius (1735–1804) and John Nost Sartorius (1759–after 1824). About these artists Oliver Millar has written, '. . . The art historian is faced for the first time with genuinely primitive painters whose work reveals almost nothing of the usual influences to which he can peg a thesis.'[5] This remark clearly explains the difficulties of writing about vernacular painting, but also illuminates the limitations of conventional art history.

In addition to hunting, shooting and fishing were also portrayed. In the nineteenth century, however, the cruelty of some sports became recognized, but the prohibition of cock-fighting in 1849 led to a sport known as 'ratting', and a growth in the interest in boxing. In the eighteenth century

boxing was attended by Royalty, but in the nineteenth century its
71 supporters were 'the lowest and least reputable class of the population' and
in many counties the sport was banned. In the 1860s the English
champion Tom Sayers prompted 'a strange revival of the pugilistic spirit'
which a number of naive artists were to record.[6]

The leisure activities of the masses were, for reasons of cost, largely
confined to spectator sports with the exception of the great feasts beloved by
Victorians and organized in the country by the gentry, or in large towns by
44 street democracy to celebrate some great public event. The *Election in
Blackburn Market Place* by an unknown painter, and the *Luncheon in Dean's
63 Pasture, Ely* by J. W. H. Southby (1801–80), show how effectively simple
artists were able to record these complex crowd scenes. At the time of
writing only this one painting by Southby, who was Verger of Ely
Cathedral and brewer to the Dean and Chapter, has been recorded.[7]
61 Walter Greaves's *Hammersmith Bridge on Boat Race Day* (*c.* 1862) is justly
renowned. Greaves's father Charles was a waterman and boatbuilder in
Chelsea who used to row Turner about the Thames. In 1847 the Greaves
family moved from 31 Cheyne Walk to 9 Lindsey Row (now 103 and
104 Cheyne Walk). It was in 1863 that Whistler moved into 7 Lindsey
Row (96 Cheyne Walk), and the subsequent paintings by Walter
Greaves and his brother Henry were doomed to lose their naive
immediacy. In Walter's words they 'went mad over Whistler', and when
not producing rather stiff townscapes of great topographical interest simply
62 aped Whistler's *Nocturnes*.[8]

49,50 Opposite, sporting scenes on japanned
tin trays were sometimes the work of
journeyman artists: top, *Hare and Hounds*,
c. 1840; below, *Pheasant Shooting, c.* 1840,
probably after an aquatint by Henry Alken.

51 Overleaf, a fourfold screen, probably from
the north of England, 1746, oil on canvas, 6 ft
6 in. high and divided into eight panels of fox-
hunting, cock-fighting, card-playing, horse-
riding, shooting, fishing, dicing, and moonlight
bathing (with voyeur at right).

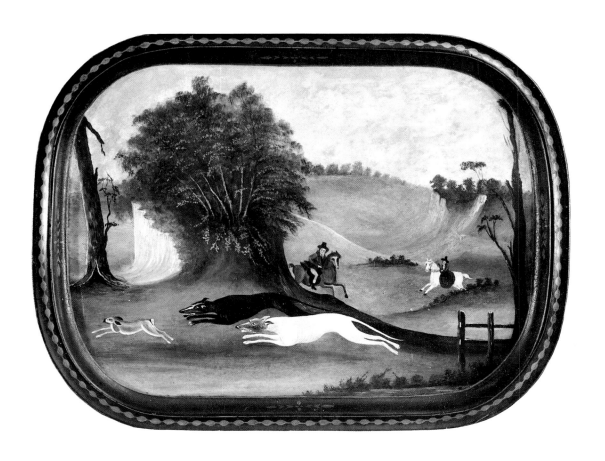

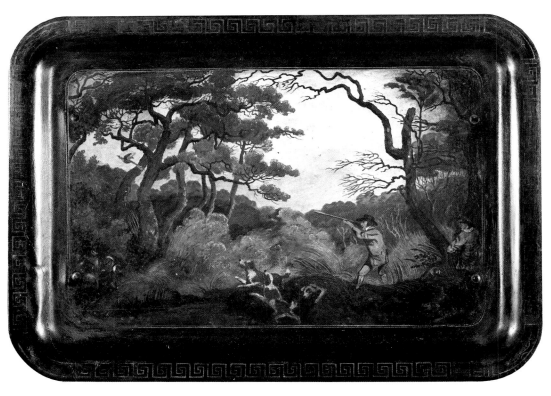

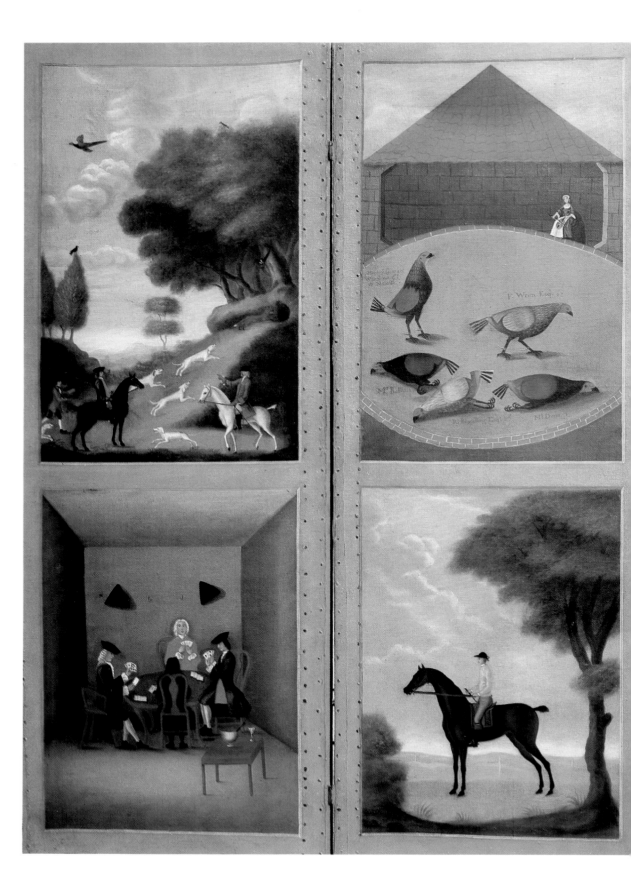

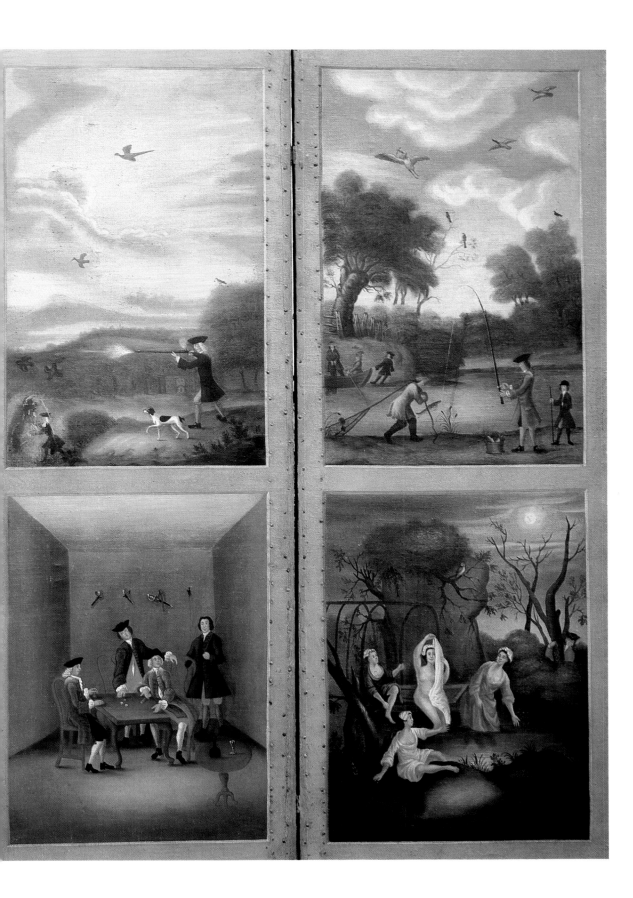

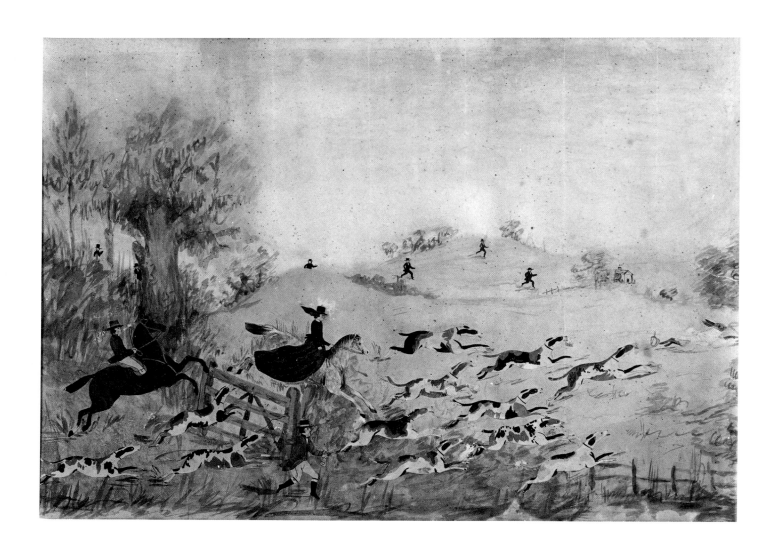

52,53,54 Three hunting scenes: above, *The Hunt*, *c.* 1850, watercolour on paper. The horses, riders and hounds, pursuing a very large hare, have been pasted down on the landscape – a convenient method for an amateur. Opposite above, *A Difficult Fence*, by J. Baker, late eighteenth century, oil on canvas; below, *A Hunt in Full Cry*, by William Meagher, 1745, oil on canvas.

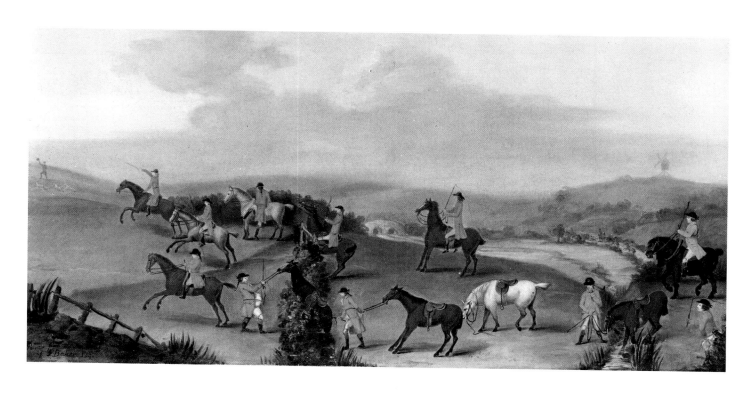

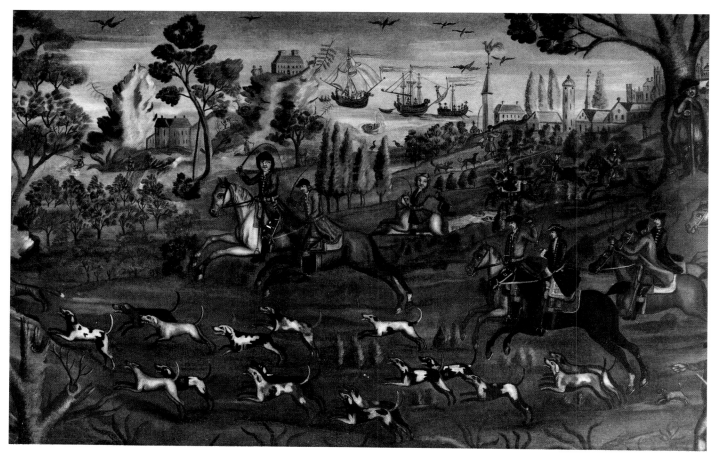

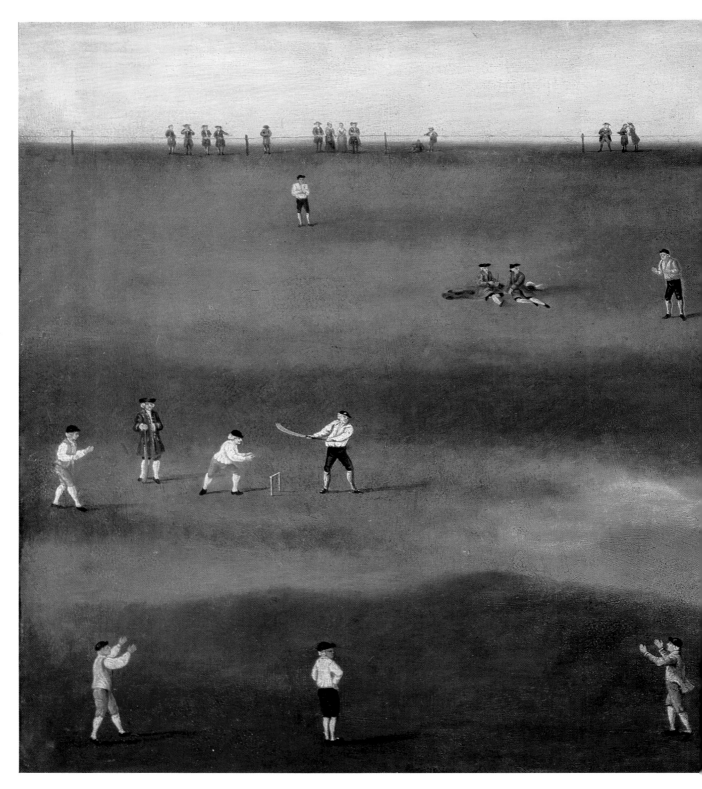

55,56,57 Above, *The Cricket Match*, attributed
to W. R. Coates, *c.* 1750; opposite, a pair of
pictures, *c.* 1870, *Boy with Kite* and *Boy with
Cricket Bat.*

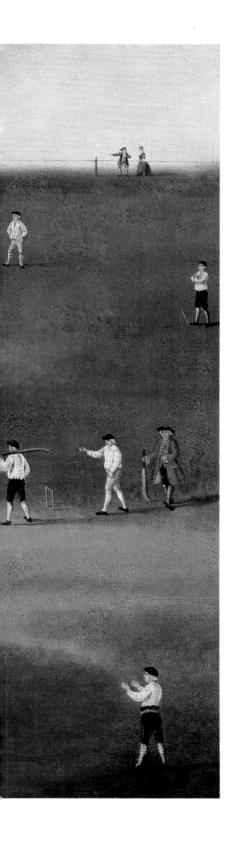

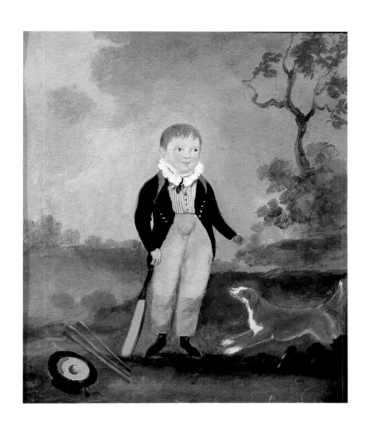

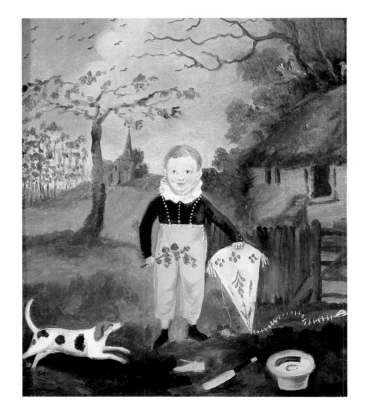

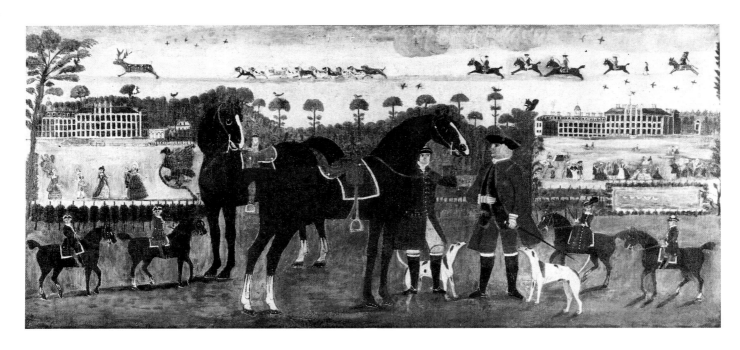

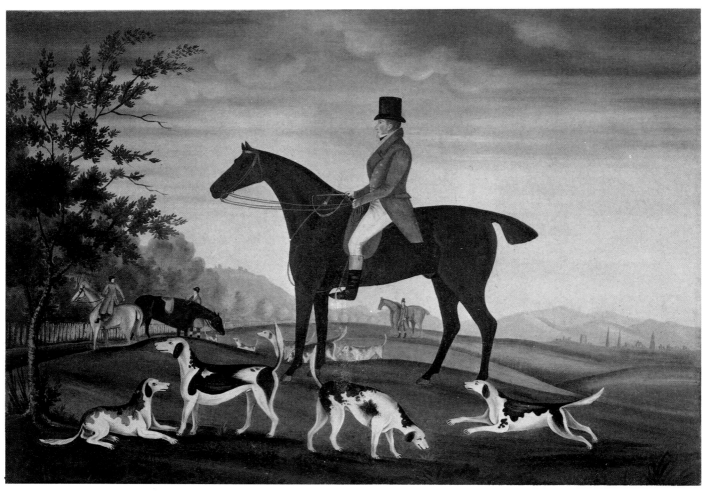

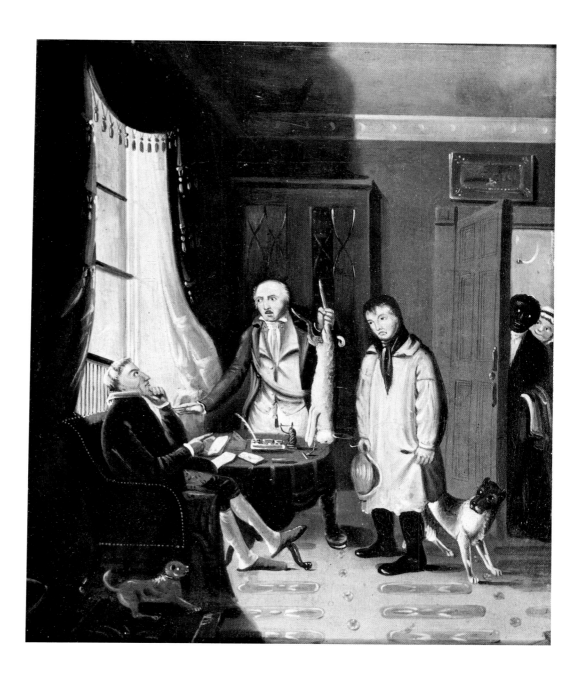

58,59 Opposite above, *The Stag Hunt*, 1781,
oil on canvas. The building in the background,
which is repeated, seems to be based on Joannes
Kip's engraving of Kensington Palace in
Britannia Illustrata (1708). Below, *A Huntsman
with Hounds*, mid nineteenth century, oil on
canvas.

60 *The Poacher*, early nineteenth century, oil on
panel.

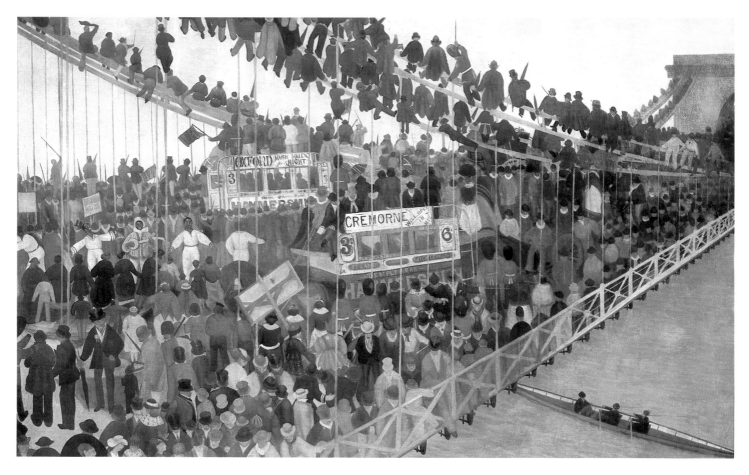

61,62 Two oil paintings by Walter Greaves
(1846–1930): above, *Hammersmith Bridge on Boat
Race Day*, painted in 1862 when Greaves was
sixteen, is both 'naive' and in twentieth-century
terms highly sophisticated. *Thames Nocturne*,
below, painted after he had been 'improved' by
James McNeill Whistler, demonstrates the
impact of the academic on the non-academic
artist.

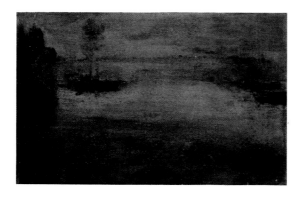

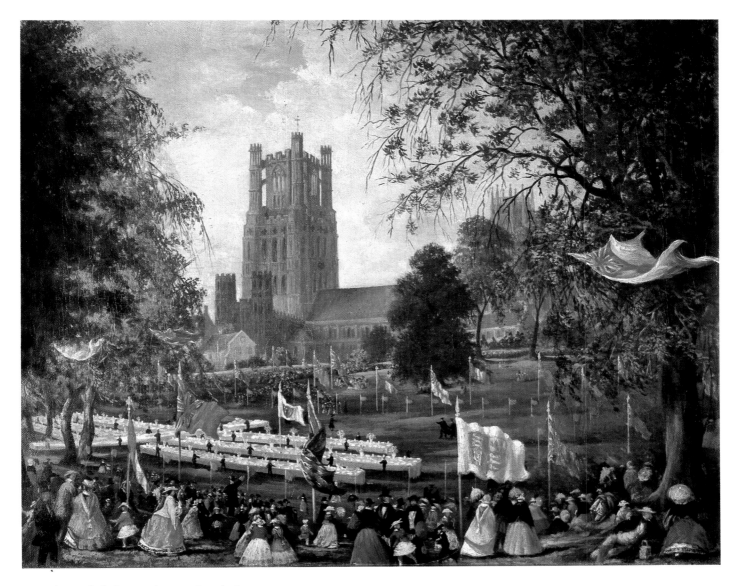

63 *Ely Cathedral: Luncheon in Dean's Pasture on
the occasion of the marriage of Princess Alexandra to
Prince Albert Edward, 1863*, by J. W. H. Southby
(1801–80), oil on canvas. Southby was Verger
of the Cathedral for sixty years, and also brewer
of ale and small beer for the Dean and Chapter.

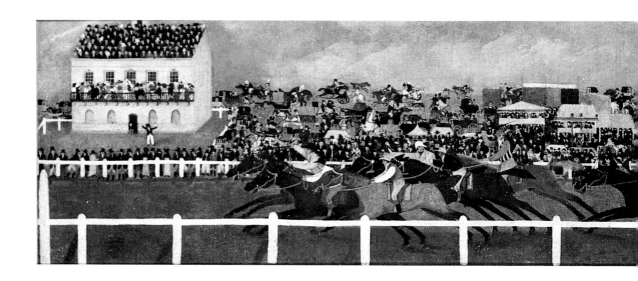

64,65,66 Naive art and 'the Sport of Kings':
above, *The Race Course*, c. 1850, oil on canvas;
below, *A Race Horse with the Jockey up*, late
eighteenth century; opposite, *The Winner's
Enclosure*, mid nineteenth century, oil on canvas.

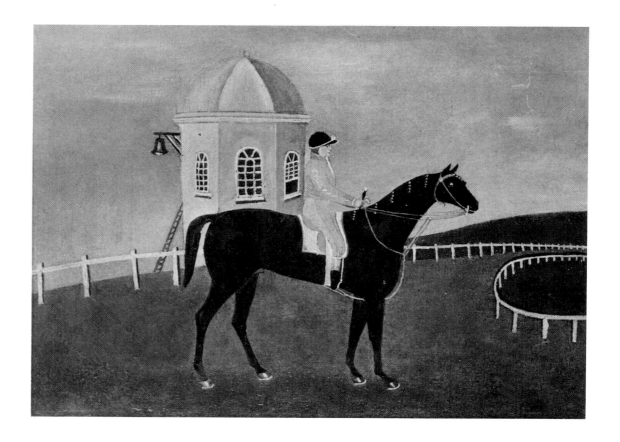

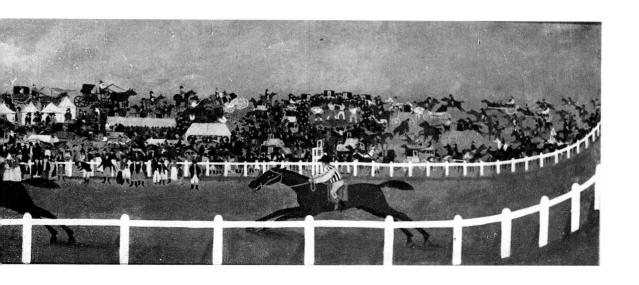

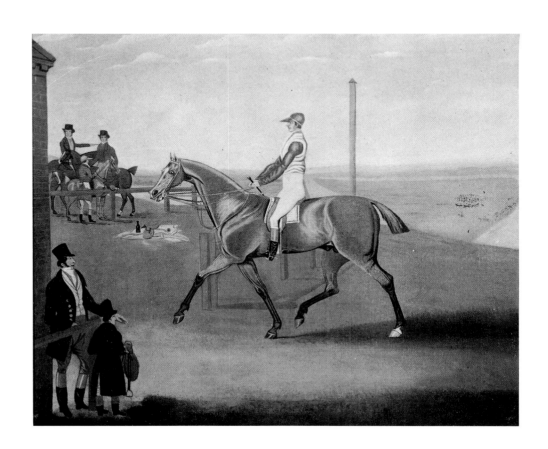

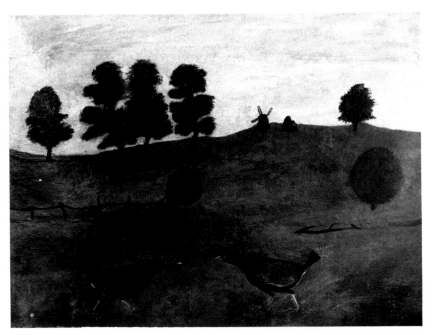

67 *Irish Fighting Cocks*, by R. Brown, 1872, oil on board. Cock-fighting was prohibited by law in Great Britain in 1849 but persisted in remote areas.

68 Below, *Nell, the Rat-hunter*, by John Whitehead, 1852, oil on canvas. The artist, who painted at least one other version of this picture, was probably a licensed victualler at the Blue Bell in Moston, near Failsworth, Lancs, according to the contemporary Manchester *Directories*.

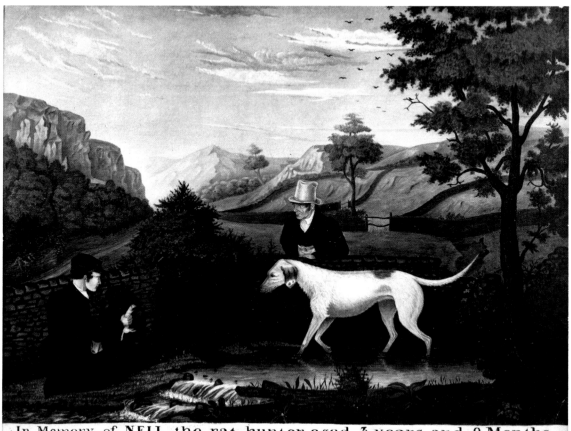

In Memory of NELL the rat-hunter, aged 3 years and 9 Months.

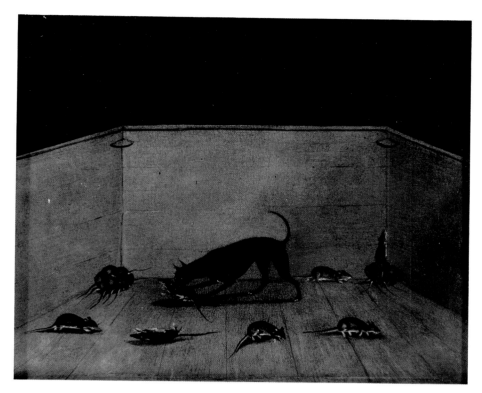

69 Above, *The Rat Pit, c.* 1855, oil on board possibly based on an engraving from Mayhew's *London Labour and the London Poor* (1851), where the pit is described as having 'a high wooden rim that reaches to elbow height'.

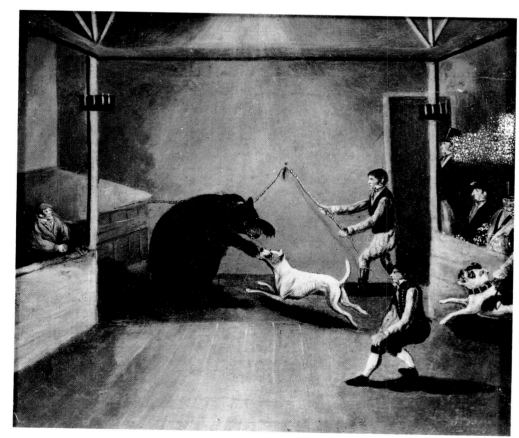

70 *Bear Baiting*, mid nineteenth century, oil on canvas. This sport had been prohibited since 1835, so the painting may record an illegal programme being held indoors and by artificial light.

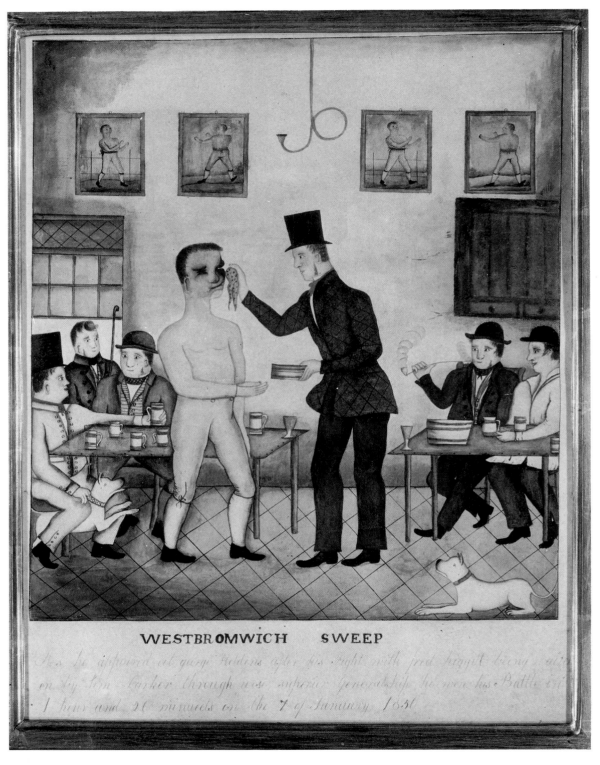

WESTBR OMWICH   SWEEP

As he appeared at george feldens after his fight with fred Naggit being beaton by Tom Barker through wis superior Generalship he won his Battle in 1 hour and 26 minuets on the 7 of January 1851

71 *The West Bromwich Sweep*, c. 1850, watercolour, painted when 'people of influence and respectability' had lost interest in the prize ring. But the 1860 contest between Sayers and Heenan saw 'a strange revival of the pugilistic spirit'.

Rural life

WITH THE INTRODUCTION of large-scale factory production, industrialization became synonymous with urbanization. By 1831 the proportion of the British population concerned with industrial and commercial activities had risen to 45 per cent, and by the third quarter of the nineteenth century more than half the population of England lived in towns.[1] It is therefore inevitable that many of the paintings illustrated in this book represent a pre-urban way of life. The country provided sustenance; it also provided and sustained a number of leisure pursuits. Today we may wish not to face some of our urban truths, and these vernacular paintings afford us a glimpse of a genuinely rural past. The landscapes are not softened by a Claudian veil of light, nor are their compositions constrained by an awareness of the ordered world of Poussin which would have disciplined the figures (even in a Rape of the Sabines) and organized the perspective. In place of these elegiac offerings we are given a view of England's past untainted by the Grand Tour.

Richard Wilson (1714–82) is often referred to as the father of English landscape painting. In the academic sense there is some truth in this assertion. But landscapes of sorts were of course painted much earlier, and from the late seventeenth century and into at least the first third of the eighteenth century they will often be found occupying the panel over the

81

chimney breast of a room. These 'Tabernacle Frames', as Batty Langley described them,[2] formed but part of a scheme of panelling in a room, and are at this period framed up with bolection mouldings; the panel within being at first flat and later 'fielded'. The landscapes that so often appear on these panels are seen from a bird's eye view. Among those who established the convention in England were a number of continental artists, among them Leonard Knyff (1650–1721), Jan Siberechts (1627–1703) and P. Tillemans (1684–1734).[3] All these artists did work for members of the British aristocracy, painting their estates with all but the detail afforded by a map. Among the English artists who adopted the convention were T. Smith with his view of Badminton from the south (c. 1700) and J. Clevely with his Ipswich river scene, which is as late as 1753. In fact the word 'landscape', which in the eighteenth century was often spelt 'landskip', derives from the Dutch landschap. The more sophisticated painters were possessed of a knowledge of perspective sufficient to create an isometric projection which combined with realism the conflicting demands of a plan of an estate with an elevation of its house. In the early eighteenth century the demand for this type of painting seems to have exceeded the number of artists capable of handling the subject with optical reality. Accordingly many delightful 'failures' survive to this day, some remaining in situ in quite elegant surroundings. Urchfont Manor in Wiltshire has an almost complete set of overmantel pictures of c. 1690. They show the house surrounded by a formal garden. The artist, as was so often the case in these vernacular landscapes, has wisely painted his view from a lower vantage point than that favoured by Knyff and others, so that the distortion is less than would otherwise have been the case. Besides, smaller houses were the focus of smaller estates with less land to display ostentatiously.

In general the 'furnishing picture', be it overmantel, overdoor or fireboard, seems not to have been considered quite seriously as art. These paintings were more connected with general painting and decorating techniques such as the graining, marbling or simulated tortoiseshell that was promiscuously applied to panelling in the first half of the eighteenth century and earlier. Furnishing pictures were contemptuously dismissed by many academic artists. Edwards says of William Williams that he 'painted Landscapes . . . in the neighbourhood of London . . . They were in general extremely harsh and tasteless, little calculated to please the eye of the connoisseur, but sufficient to answer the purpose of those who sought for paintings as furniture.'[4]

The landscape for its own sake is seldom a feature of early or primitive painting, and it usually occurs in naive painting as a background. The foreground is often painted with some care, although certain devices were adopted and became conventionalized. An example of this 'reflex' painting occurs wherever water is shown, for floating on its surface will often be found a symbol which is little more than a cypher signifying a 'swan'. This punctuation of the composition may be seen in the foreground of the exceptionally primitive *Daisy and her Calf*, in the *Landscape with Exotic Buildings*, and in the coaching scene. An explanation for this may be found in Nathaniel Whittock's *The Oxford Drawing Book* (1825) which states that 'swans . . . are frequently introduced into aquatic scenery with the happiest effect'.

'Flower pieces' in watercolour or in other materials were often made as a 'ladies' accomplishment'. Stencil pictures on velvet were popular, but in *The Female Student* (1836) Mrs Phelps warned that though 'handsome pictures are made . . . they are almost wholly mechanical operations.' The still life which shows the produce of the land is rare. Rural activities are represented by hop picking, which in Kent traditionally and until the 1950s provided a working holiday for Londoners. The painting of a *Country Fete*, which refers to 'Strawberries and Cream', could also be from the Garden of England, a reputation Kent acquired as early as 1697 when Celia Fiennes noted, 'Kentish Cherry's a good sort of Flemish fruite'.[5]

The recurrence of the inn or public house as a subject may be due either to its central social role in village life or it may point to inn-sign painters extending their income. Carriage painters often furnished stage-coach doors with representations of the signs of the inns from which they operated, and this may suggest that such paintings were the work of carriage painters.[6]

108
81, 87
72
84
87

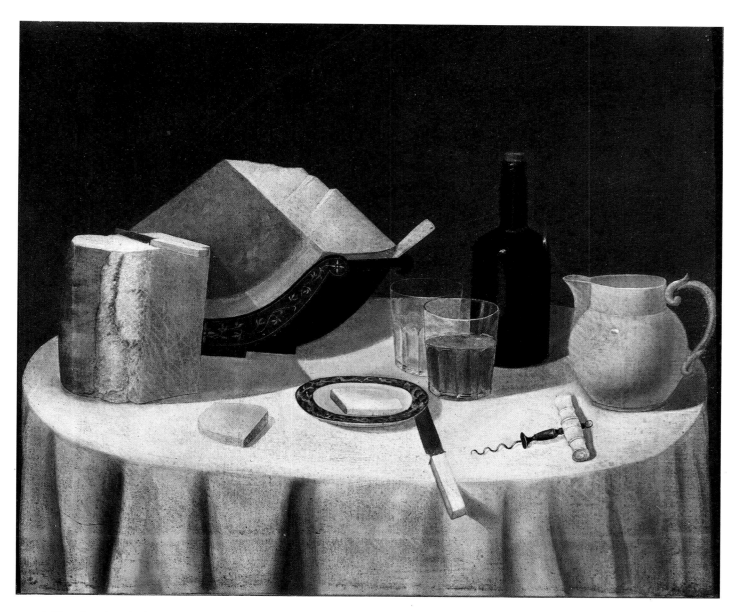

72 *Still Life with Cheshire Cheese*, by J. B.
Higginson, 1869, oil on canvas. The cheese is
provided with a cheese cradle, and the
corkscrew has a brush for brushing the cork.
John Booth Higginson is listed in the 1869
Directories for Madeley, Staffs, as a 'painter and
decorator'.

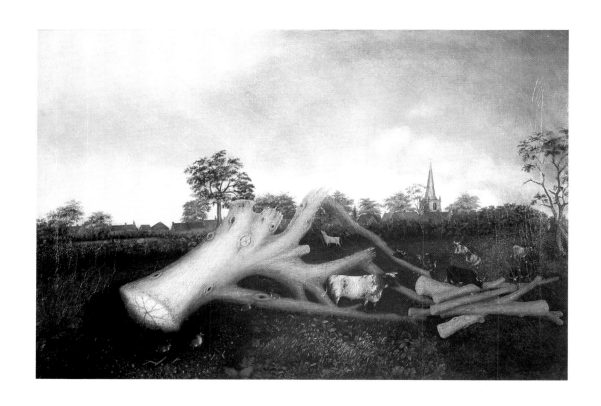

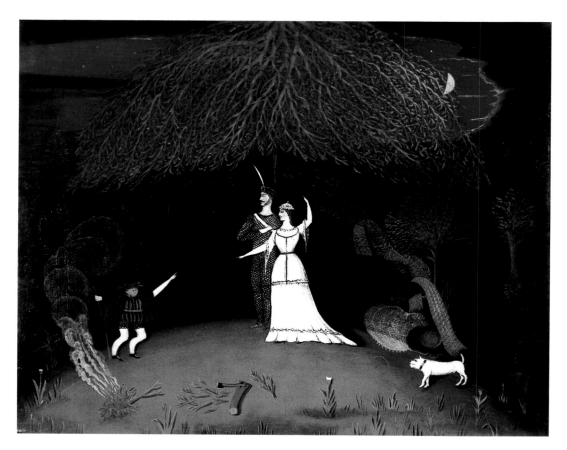

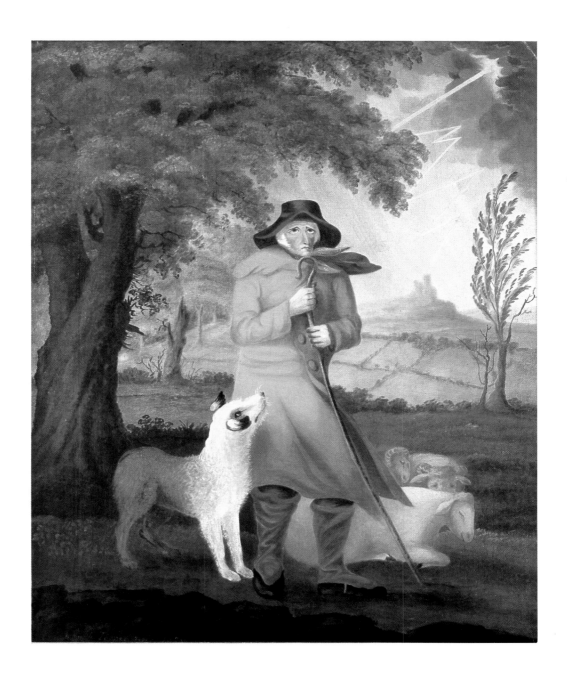

73 Opposite above, *Fallen Greatness*, by Mary Merrall, 1880, oil on canvas.

74 Opposite below, *Midsummer Night's Dream*, by W. Balls, *c.* 1860, oil on canvas. The ethereal quality of this picture is remarkable but the individual figures probably derive from cheap theatrical printed portraits.

75 *A Shepherd with an English Sheep Dog, c.* 1820, oil on canvas. The painting is inscribed 'Josia Pepper', probably the name of the shepherd.

76 *A Country Schoolroom, c.* 1850, oil on canvas.

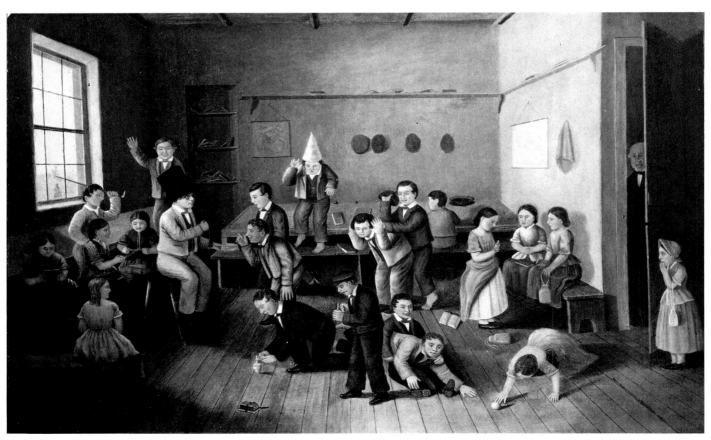

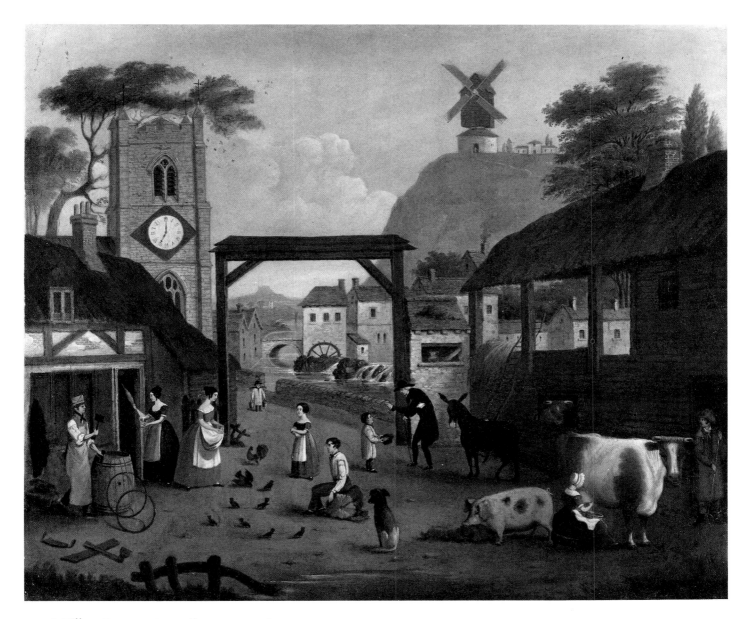

77 *A Village Street*, *c.* 1840, oil on canvas. An
amalgam of idealized rural scenes and activities,
this painting may have been derived from an
earlier picture with most of the costumes
brought up to date. The cooper on the left wears
a hat made of newspaper like the Carpenter in
Tenniel's illustration to *The Walrus and the
Carpenter.*

78 *Bringing Home the Cows*, late eighteenth century, oil on canvas:

The Curfew tolls the knell of parting day,
The lowing herd wind slowly o'er the lea . . .

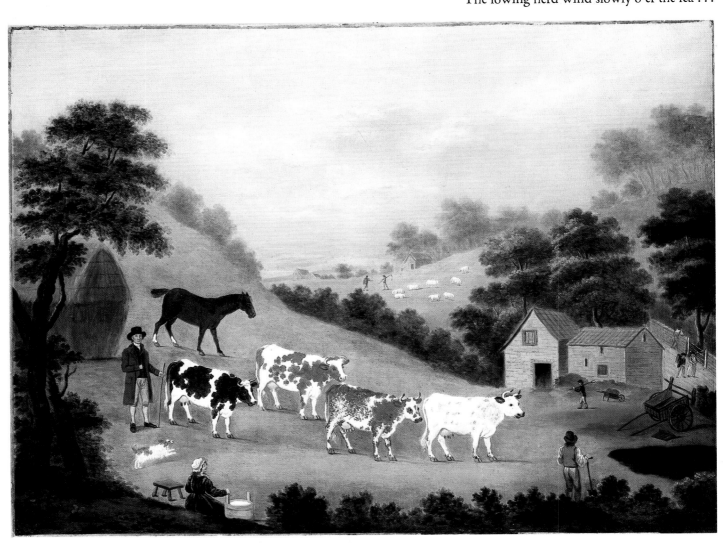

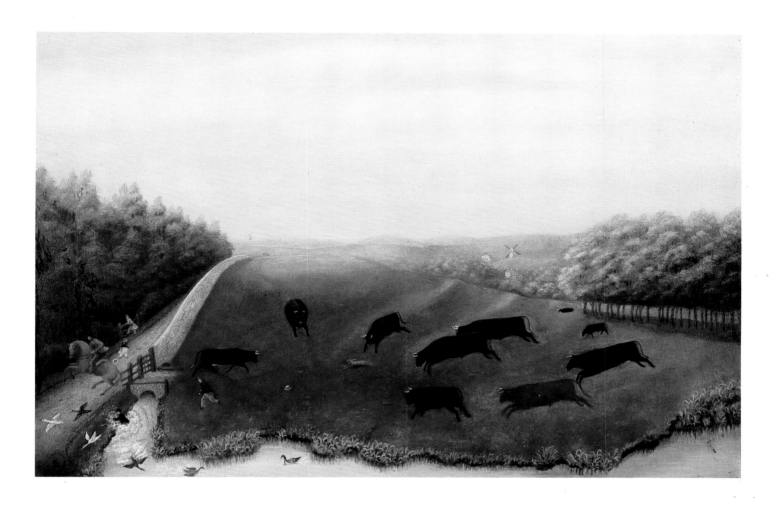

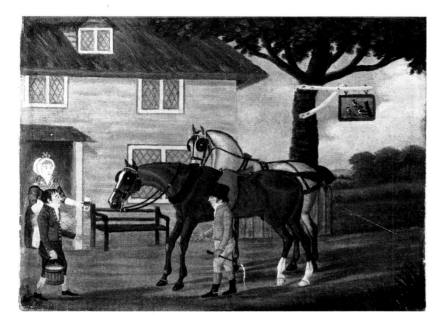

79 *Nine Angry Bulls*, oil on canvas, mid nineteenth century. The bulls converge furiously on a hare, while a rider and two walkers scramble over a stream, and a sense of panic spreads to the waterfowl and little girls in the lane.

80 *At the Magpie Inn*, by John Cordrey, early nineteenth century. Two other Cordrey paintings were exhibited in the 1967 *Primitives* exhibition in London.

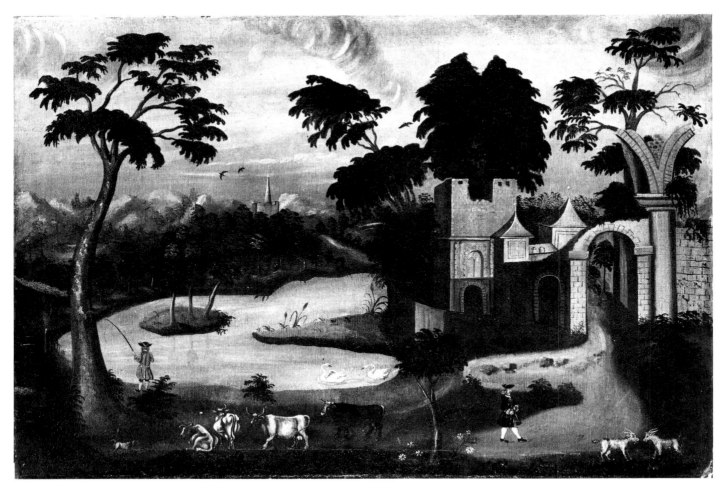

81,82,83 Three naive landscapes: above, *Landscape with Exotic Buildings*, an oil painting from the first half of the eighteenth century, is a decorative furnishing picture, painted on very coarse canvas. Opposite, a pair of *Village Scenes*, late nineteenth century, oil on cardboard. Their mood recalls Flora Thompson's *Lark Rise to Candleford.*

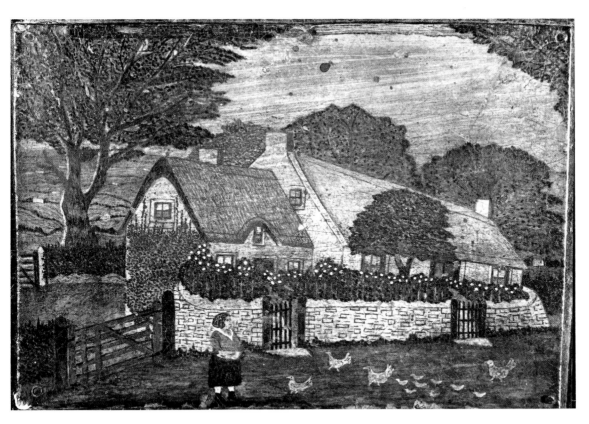
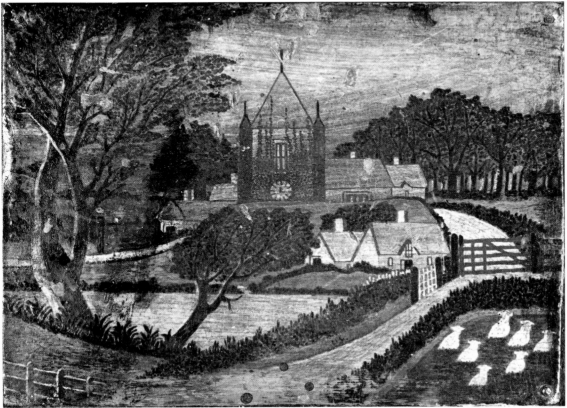

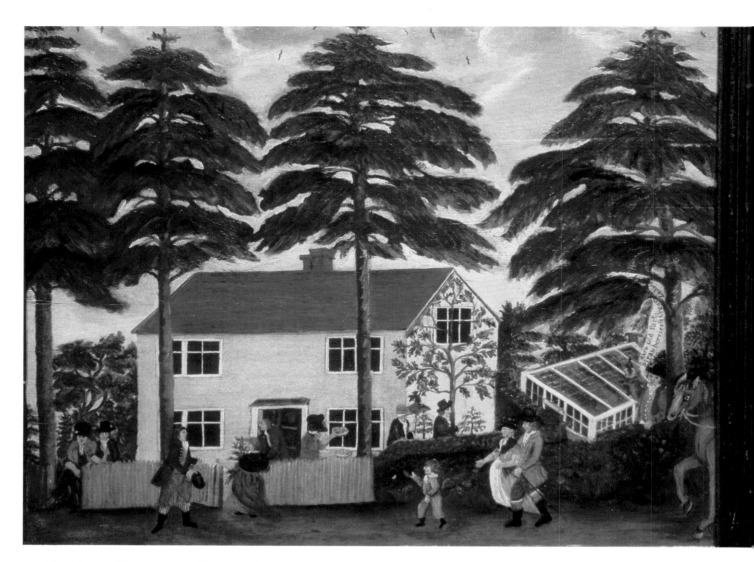

84 *The Country Fete*, *c.* 1800, oil on panel, was
originally one composition which has been
sawn down the centre. The figure on the right of
the left-hand panel is saying, 'Rare old port,
strawberries and cream, ladies.'

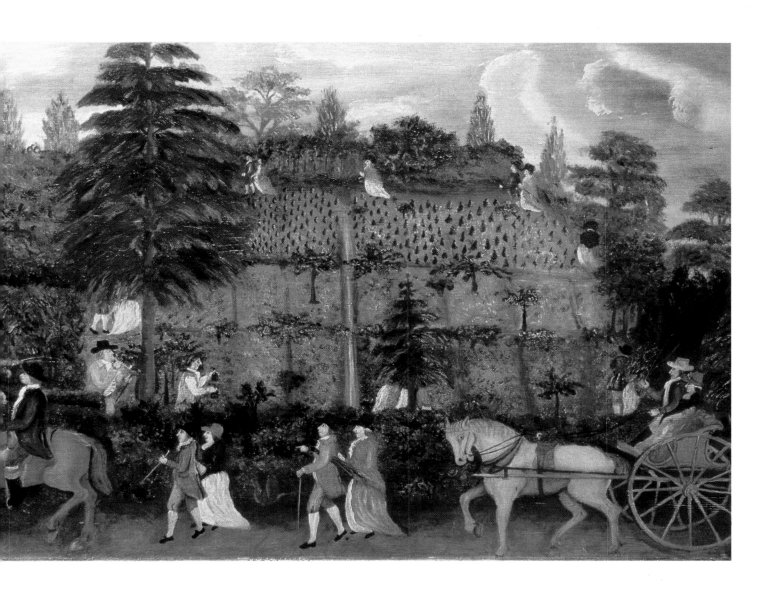

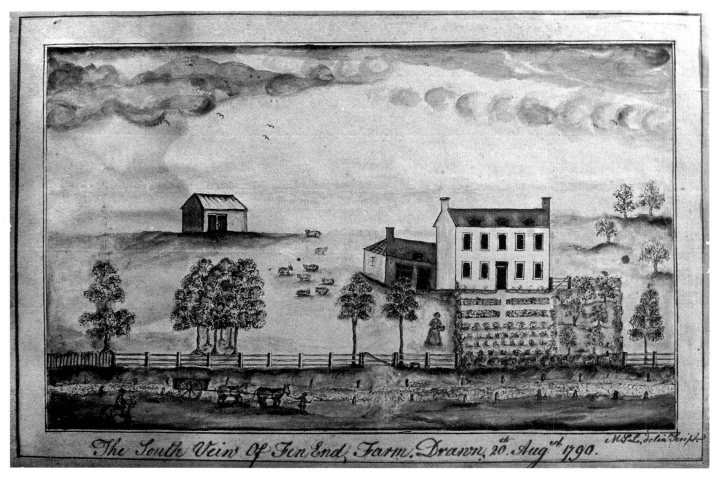

The South View Of Fen End, Farm. Drawn 20th Augᵗ 1790.

85,86 Above, *South View of Fen End Farm*, 1790, watercolour. Information contained in naive topographical views may usually be relied upon, since they seldom 'improved' compositions. In the painting opposite, however, *William Buckenham, Linen Manufacturer's Cart*, the artist has provided the flat county of Norfolk with a remarkably mountainous landscape.

87 Opposite below, *Stagecoach arriving at the White Lion*, early nineteenth century, oil on canvas, possibly by a carriage or sign painter attempting to extend his range of work. The carved bear represented on the side of the coach is still to be seen at The Bear, Devizes, one of the town's principal inns.

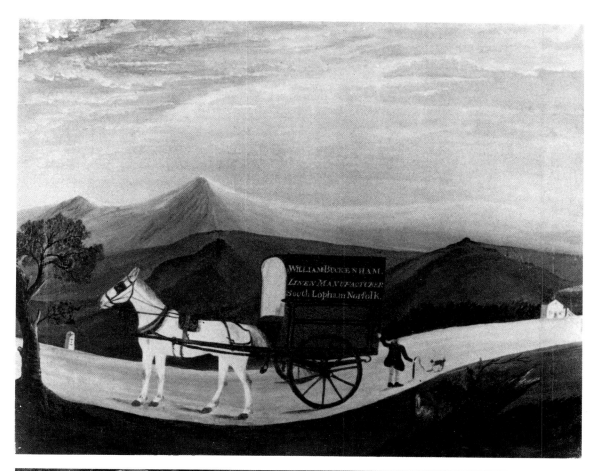

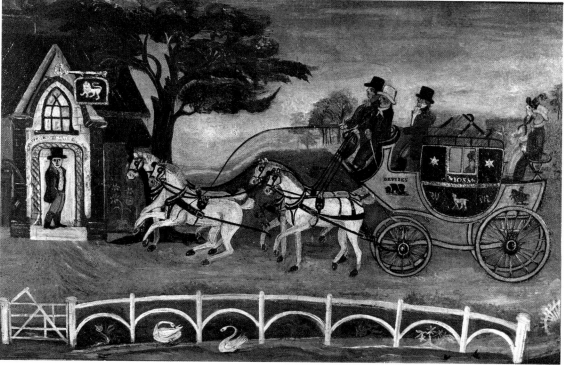

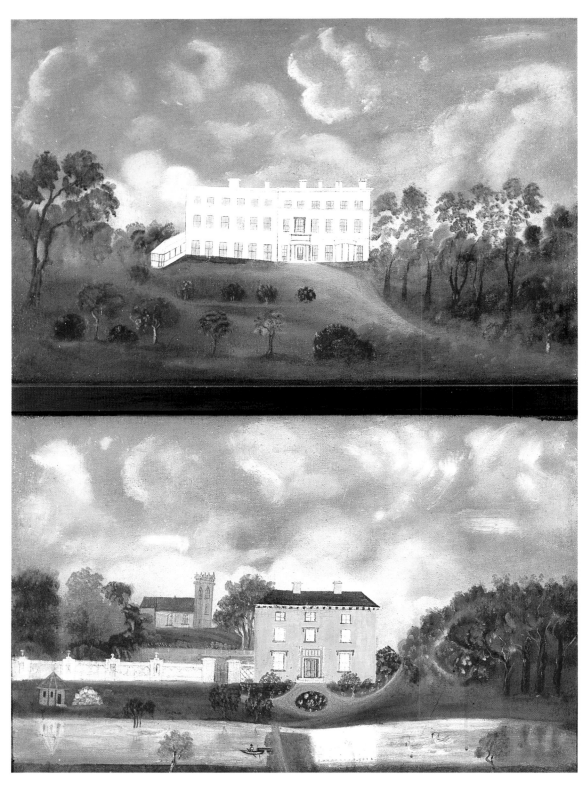

88,89,90,91 *Four Country Houses*, *c.* 1840, oil on canvas. These 'casement pictures' by an

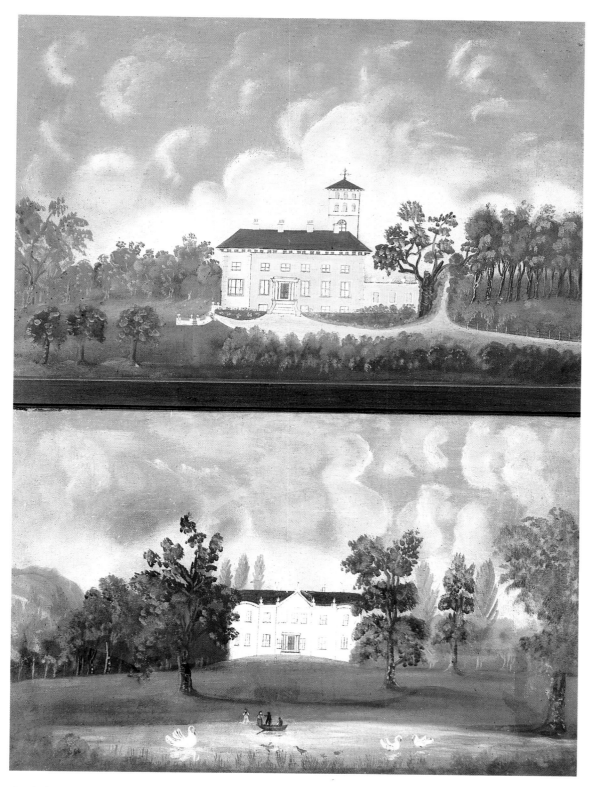

English artist were found inside the wooden
interior shutters of a New England house.

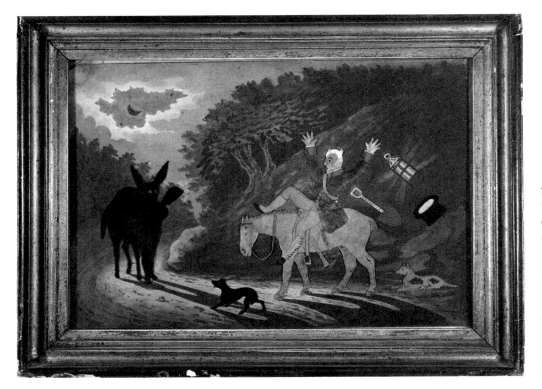

92 *The Earth Stopper*, by George Smart, second quarter of nineteenth century, a fabric collage on paper with watercolour. The earth stopper (employed to stop up foxes' earths before the hunt) meets the village sweep and 'takes him for the Devil.' Smart reproduced this composition many times.

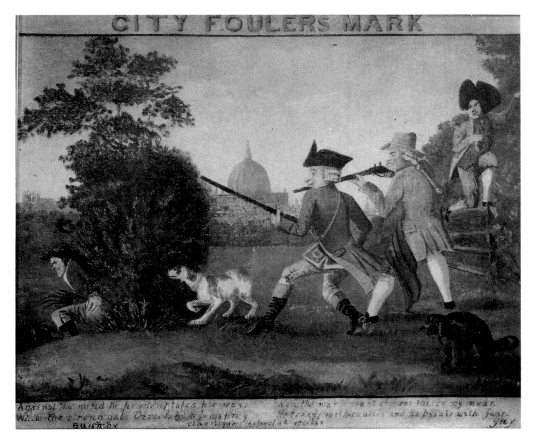

CITY FOULERS MARK

Against the wind he prudent takes his way.
While the strong gale Directs his to his prey.
GUILFOY

Now the war..geant desires this coney near.
He treads with caution and he spies with fear.
clam itique exspect at oredlas
Gay

93 *City Foulers Mark*, c. 1750, oil on board. London and St Paul's are visible on the skyline. The verse is from John Gay's *Trivia*.

Birds and beasts

And Adam gave names to all cattle, and to the fowl of the air and to every beast of the field. *Genesis, ii, 20*

It is perhaps appropriate that in a book on this primary art there should be
94, 149 two items illustrating the theme of Adam naming the birds and beasts. In general, however, it was the practical demands of livestock breeders that gave rise to animal portraits, whilst the need for something purely
103, 105 decorative was often met by bird pictures. Many of the paintings of livestock have a splendid power which is quite distinct from the charm of the pictures of domesticated animals by amateurs. This charm even extends to W. H. Rogers's painting of the *Lion Tamer* with a lion, tiger and
95 'ligers'. Sporting dogs seem to have been painted by professional artists of the type more often employed to portray race horses and hunters.

The first patrons of this art of representing in pictures superlative examples of the animal kingdom were almost exclusively interested in the horse. A life-size portrait of a large grey horse, which probably once belonged to Sir Robert Cecil, was painted in 1594 and hangs to this day in Hatfield House. The interest in animal subjects other than horses does not seem to have become general until Thomas Coke of Holkham and others encouraged a more scientific approach to agriculture in the late eighteenth century. Nevertheless as early as 1697 Celia Fiennes records in her diary:

'... In the pantry [at Newby Hall] hangs a picture of the dimensions of a large ox that was fed in these grounds with the account of its weight, the quarter was 106 stone ...'[1] Many of the surviving early pictures of animals must be viewed as part of the mainstream of the art of their time, but Celia Fiennes's account suggests that the preoccupation with dimensions and weight was removing such paintings from the restricting cultural obligations of 'art' to the less stifling demands of measurement. Furthermore, the lowly status of such a picture is clearly indicated by its being hung in the pantry at a time when the pictures in the main part of Newby Hall were 'not set up, the house being in mourning' for the wife of the owner and her mother, Lady Yorke.

Throughout the first half of the nineteenth century and later the painting of farm animals became a recognized genre. A few artists such as Thomas Weaver of Shropshire (1774–1843) fall outside the parameters of this book, but most were naive in the sense that they were quite unconcerned with aesthetic considerations. Thomas Bewick, who is today so loved for his *British Birds* (1797 and 1804) and *A General History of Quadrupeds* (1790), made in 1789 a particularly fine and large wood engraving of the famous *Chillingham Wild Bull*. Bewick found the demands of some clients incompatible with his art:

After I had made my drawings from the fat sheep, I soon saw that they were not approved, but that they were to be made like certain paintings shown to me. I observed to my employer that the paintings bore no resemblance to the animals whose figures I had made my drawings from; and that I would not alter mine to suit the paintings that were shown to me ... my journey, as far as concerned these fat cattle makers, ended in nothing. I objected to put lumps of fat here and there where I could not see it, at least not in so exaggerated a way as on the painting before me; so 'I got my labour for my trouble'. Many of the animals were during this *rage* for fat cattle, fed up to as great a weight and bulk as it was possible for feeding to make them; but this was not enough; they were to be figured monstrously fat before the owners of them could be pleased. Painters were found who were quite subservient to this guidance, and nothing else would satisfy. Many of these paintings will mark the times, and, by the exaggerated productions of the artists, serve to be laughed at when the folly and the self-interested motives which gave them birth are done away.[2]

Bewick's rueful account is probably all too true, but to what extent did these animals in fact carry the remarkable weights with which they are credited? D. H. Boalch came to the conclusion that, allowing for some degree of exaggeration, in general animals were bred and fed to look as extraordinary as their portraits. Boalch goes on to say that 'sometimes these fattened beasts became too heavy for their legs and had to be shored up with timber'.[3]

These grotesques of nature corrupted by man were toured around the country as sideshows in market towns where the discerning eye of the local farmers would be duly impressed. By 1809 a pig known as the Yorkshire Hog had made as much as £3000 over a period of three years.[4] Many of the paintings of these beasts were produced for the purpose of subsequent engraving which provided a still further source of revenue.

Serious attempts to improve longhorn cattle were begun by Robert Bakewell in about 1750, and by 1755 he was also improving the Leicester sheep. *Coate's Herd Book* of 1822 for the shorthorn breed of cattle is the earliest bloodstock book and was followed much later by stud-books for heavy horses in the years 1878–80 (although some pedigrees dated back a few years earlier). The first herd-book association for pigs was the Berkshire, founded in 1884, followed by the Large and Middle White in 1885. Flock-books for sheep did not appear until after 1910. As these various publications became available so the demand for paintings of outstanding beasts declined.

Exhibitions of both prints and paintings of British farm livestock were held at Mr Augustus Walker's galleries in New Bond Street, London, in 1932 and 1934, and others appeared at the Museum of English Rural Life, Reading, in 1957 and 1979. The Museum of English Rural Life has a good collection of animal portraits, as does the Rothamsted Experimental Station, Hertfordshire.

119

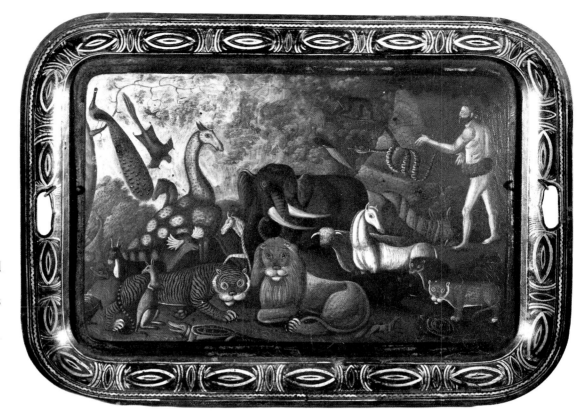

94 *Adam Naming the Birds and Beasts*, first half of nineteenth century, painted tin tray. The design of human figure with animals recalls the work of the American painter Edward Hicks (1780–1849) who repeatedly returned to the theme of *The Peaceable Kingdom*.

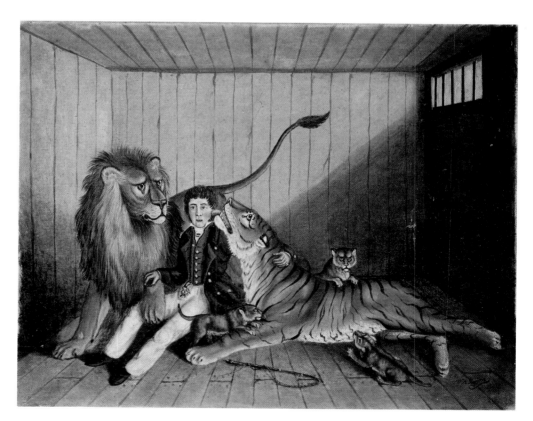

95 *The Lion Tamer*, by W. H. Rogers, mid nineteenth century, oil on canvas.

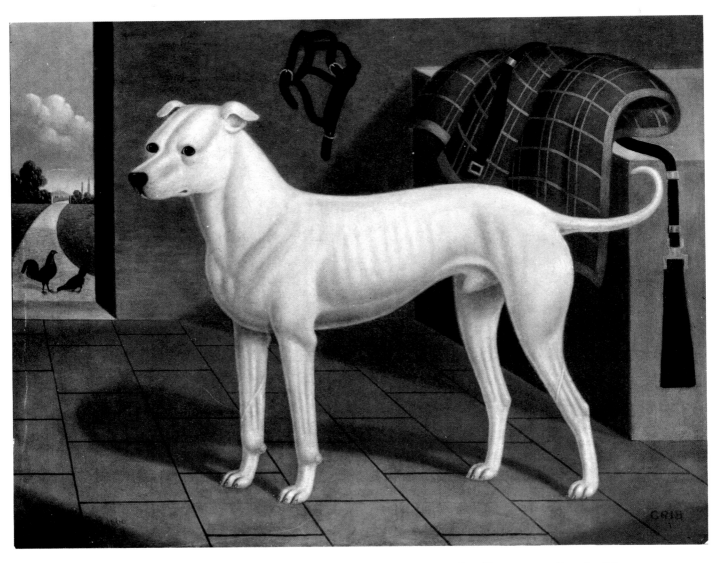

96 *'Crib'; a Sporting Dog*, by Thomas
Roebuck, 1860, oil on canvas, one of a pair.
Working dogs tended to be painted by
professional artists, while household pets were
subjects often favoured by amateurs.

97 Opposite above, *Canine Friends*, mid
nineteenth century, oil on canvas.

98,99 Opposite, a pair of watercolour-on-velvet
pictures, early nineteenth century: *The Black
Puppy* and *The Kitten*. Pictures stencilled on
velvet, popular in early nineteenth-century
America, are rare in England.

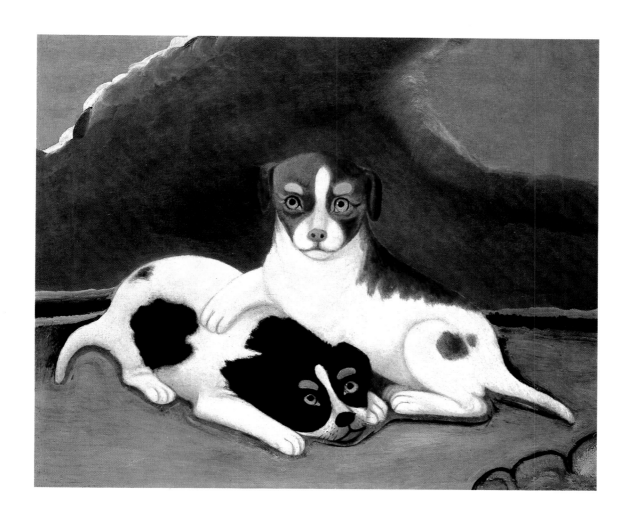

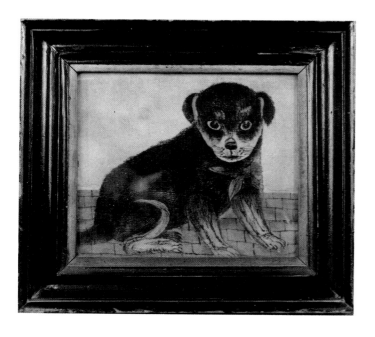

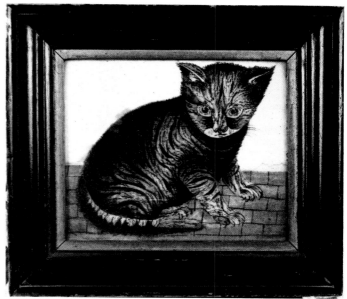

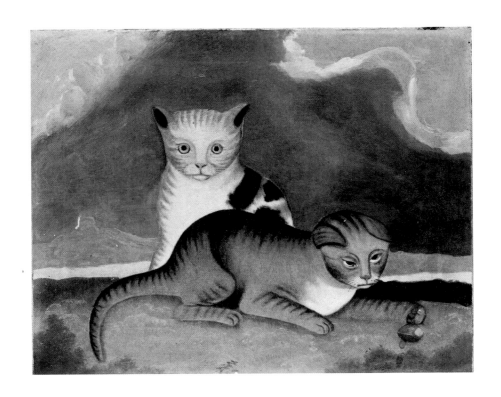

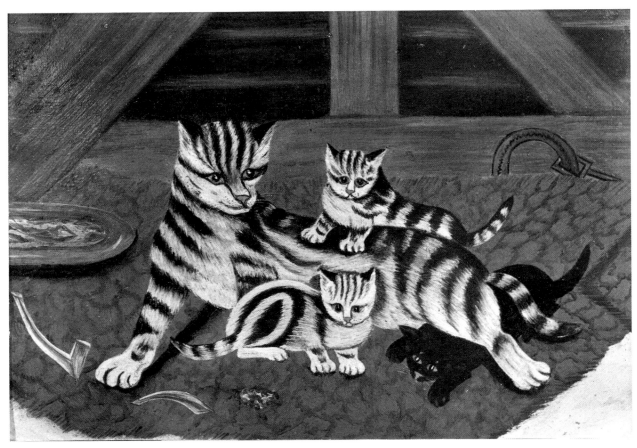

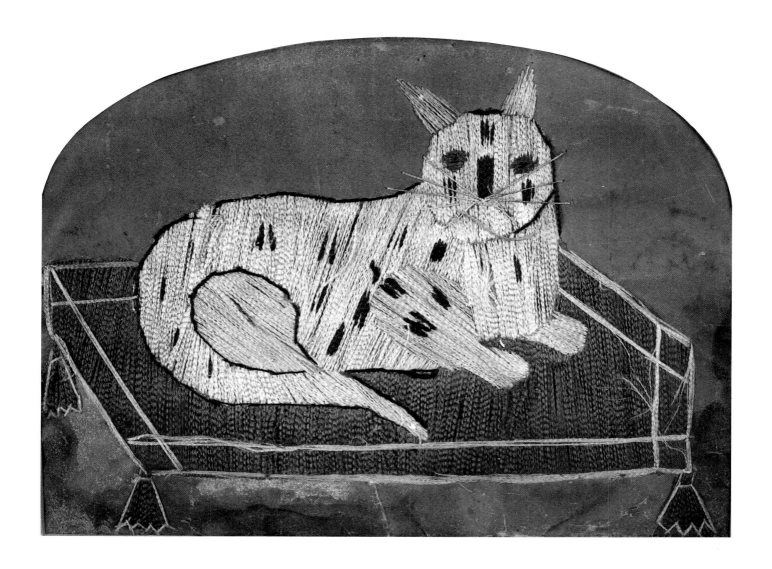

100 Opposite above, *Feline Friends*, mid
nineteenth-century oil painting, a pair to *Canine
Friends* (Pl 97).

101 Opposite, *Cat and Kittens*, late nineteenth
century, oil on metal tray.

102 Above, *A Cat on a Cushion*, an embroidery
on paper, *c.* 1875–90, which may well be the
work of a child.

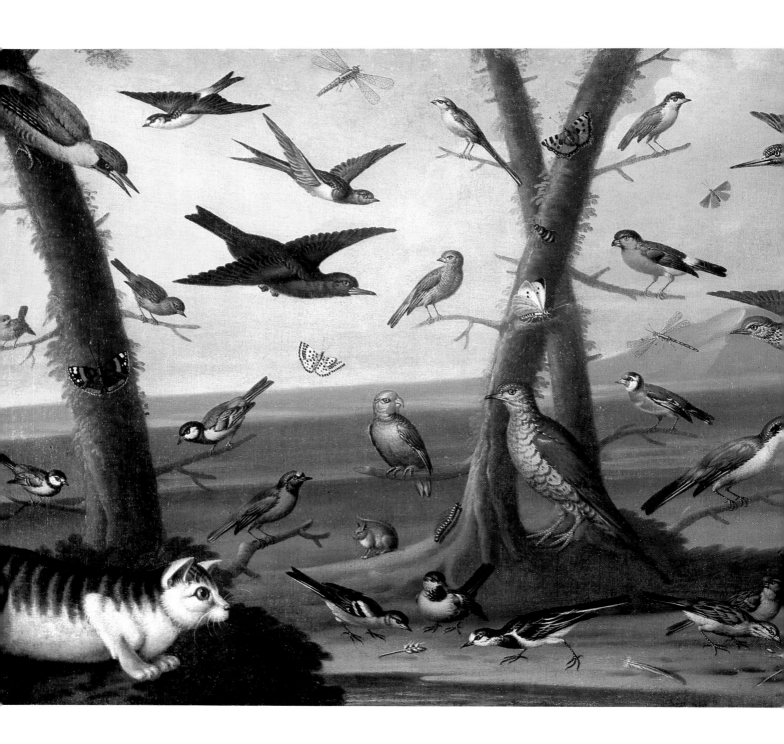

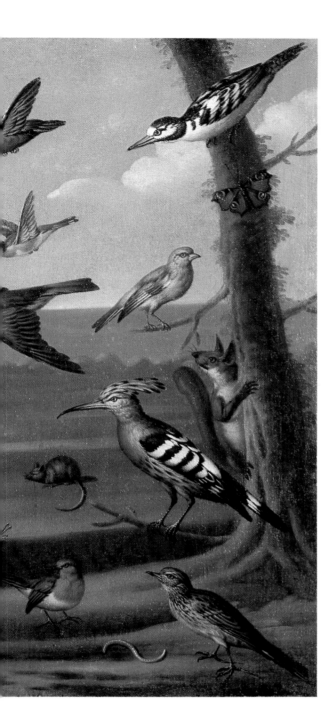

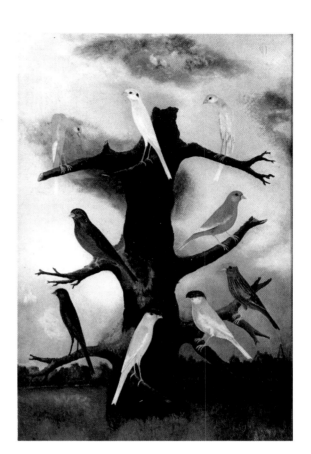

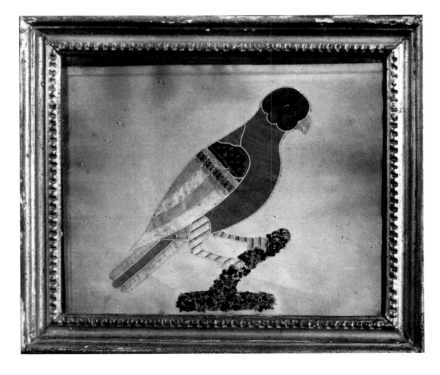

103 *A Cat among the Birds*, early eighteenth century, oil on canvas.

104,105 Above, *The Miners' Canaries*, by Hodgson, 1901, back-painted glass. Right, *The Parrot*, eighteenth century, silk, paper and mica.

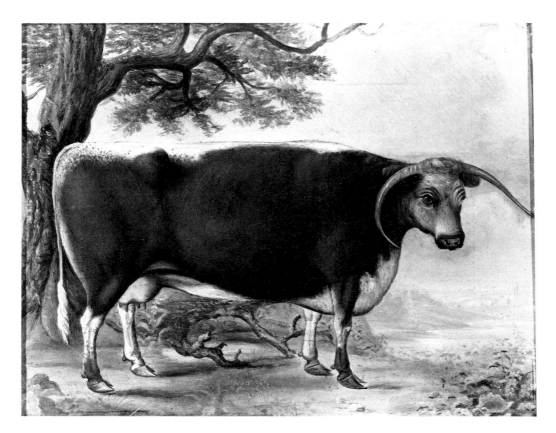

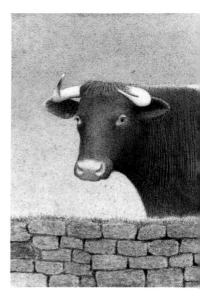

106,107 Left, *Longhorn Cow*, an early nineteenth century oil painting; below, *Captain Scarlet*, by Joseph Sheppard, *c.* 1865–70, watercolour on paper. Sheppard was a farmer's son with some artistic training.

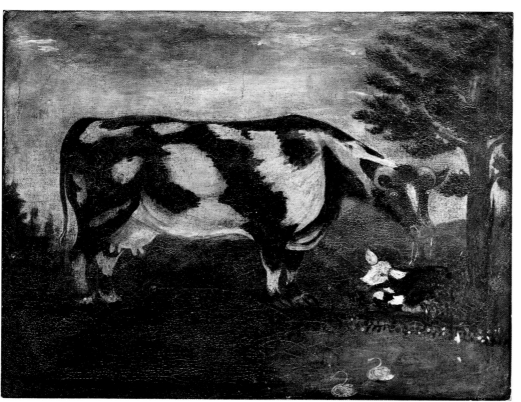

108 Left, *Daisy the Cow with her Calf*, early nineteenth century, oil on board. An inscription on the back suggests that it was painted by a 'painter and glazier'.

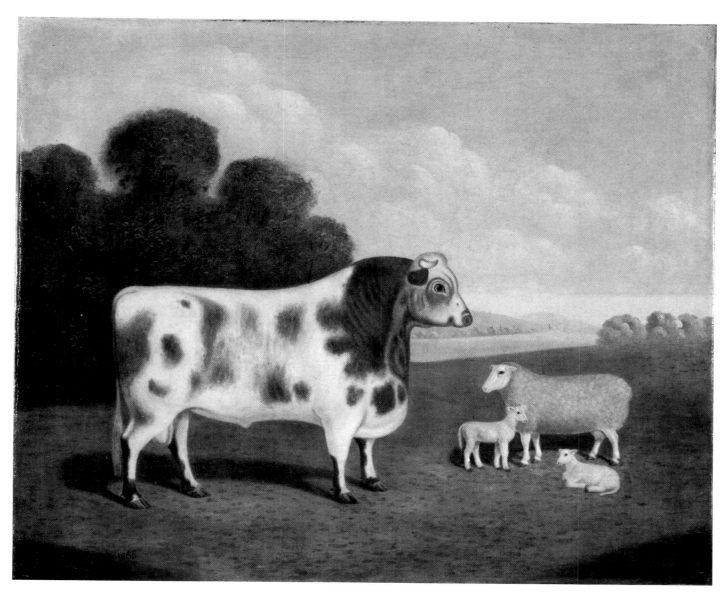

109 *A Durham Shorthorn Bull with Sheep*, by
Thomas Roebuck, 1860, oil on canvas. It was
not until the turn of the century that colour
became a fixed part of the description of a breed.
Until then there was little conformity.

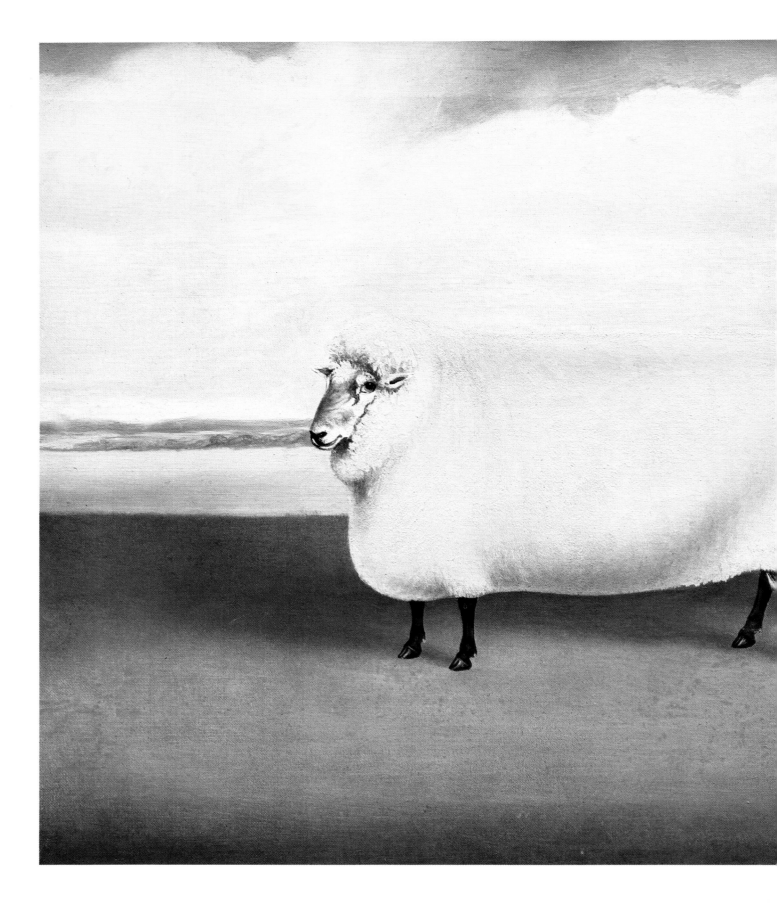

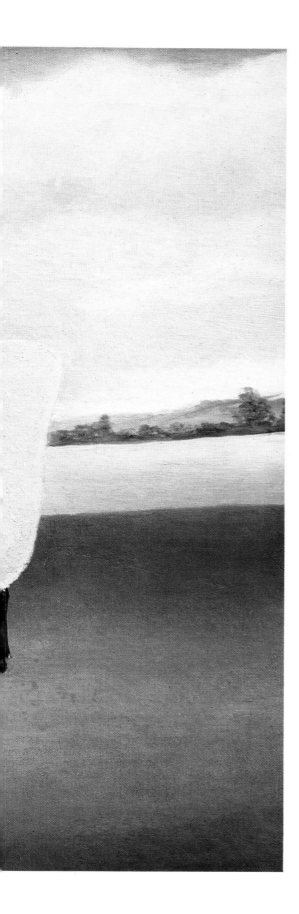

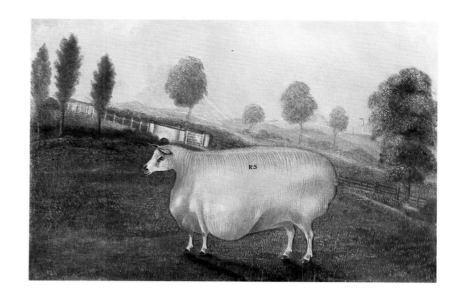

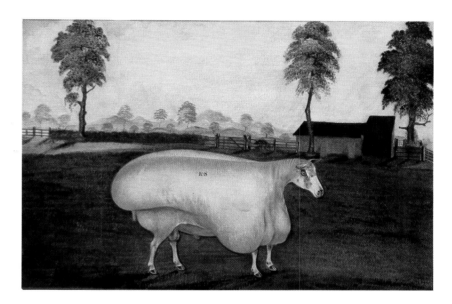

111,112 Top and above, a pair of paintings:
The White Ewe and *The White Ram* (Dishley
Leicesters) by William Bagshaw, 1846, listed in
the Rugby *Directories* under 'plumbers and
glaziers'.

110 Opposite, *The Prize Ram*, *c.* 1850, oil on
canvas. The lack of reflected light gives this
picture its heraldic power.

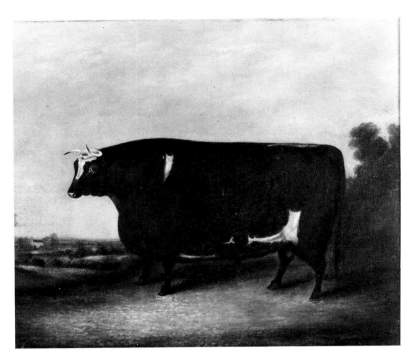

113 *The Thorney Prize Ox*, James Clark, 1858,
oil on canvas. The beast took 'First Prize in
London, £25; First Prize at Peterborough, £8;
and Second Prize at Oakham, £7, and was
sold for £65. Xmas 1858 was 4 yrs 5 months
old, weighed 128 st 8 lb, Loose fat 19 st 6 lbs.'

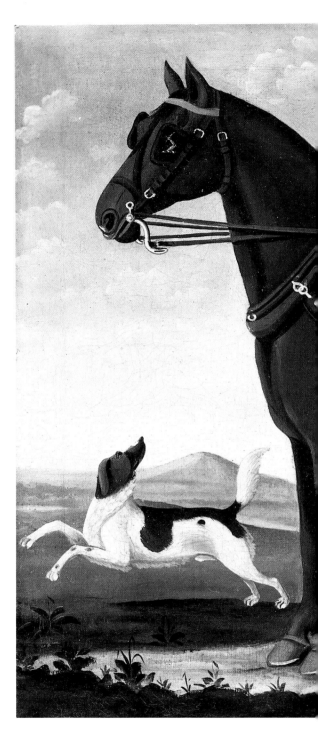

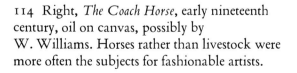

114 Right, *The Coach Horse*, early nineteenth
century, oil on canvas, possibly by
W. Williams. Horses rather than livestock were
more often the subjects for fashionable artists.

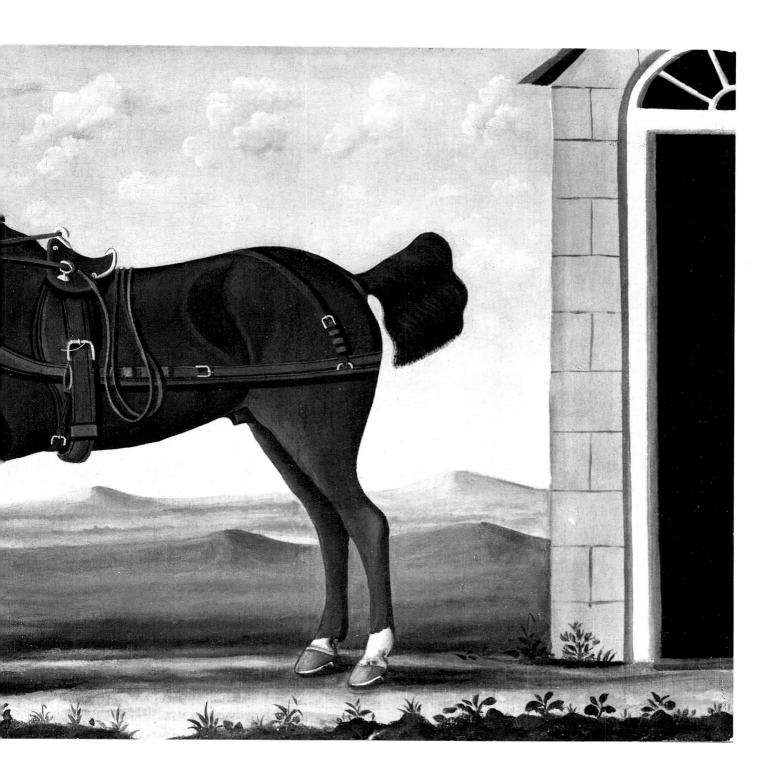

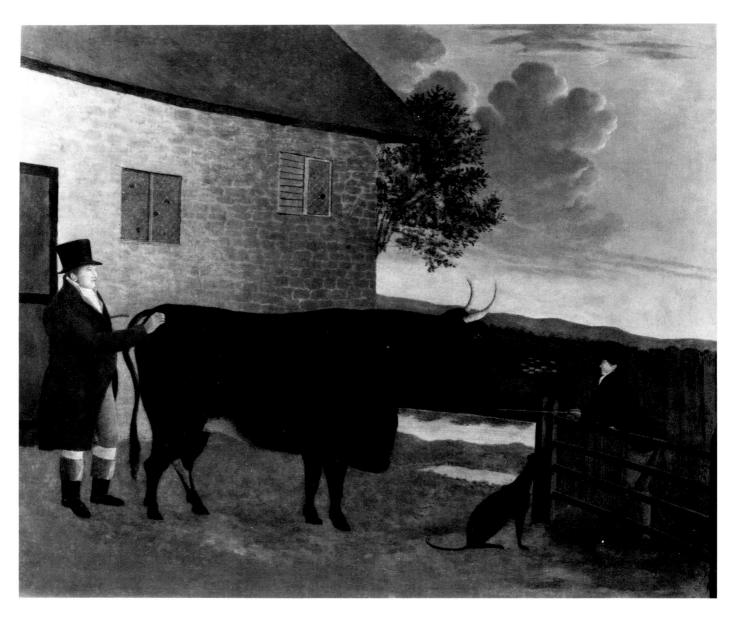

115 Above, *A Farmer with Prize Bull, c.* 1830, oil on canvas. The beast shown here may be a Kerry.

116,117 Opposite above, *A Prize Bull and a Prize Cabbage*, by W. Williams, 1804; below, *A Farmer and Prize Heifer*, early nineteenth century. The clients demanded that the cattle be painted 'monstrously fat'.

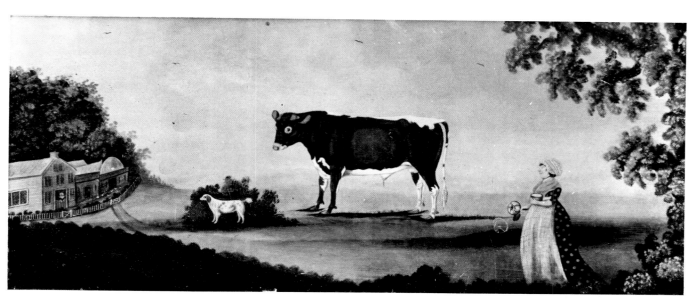

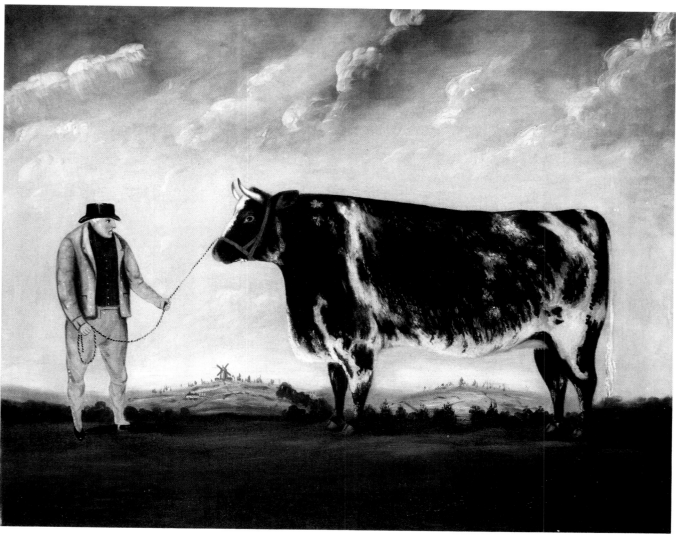

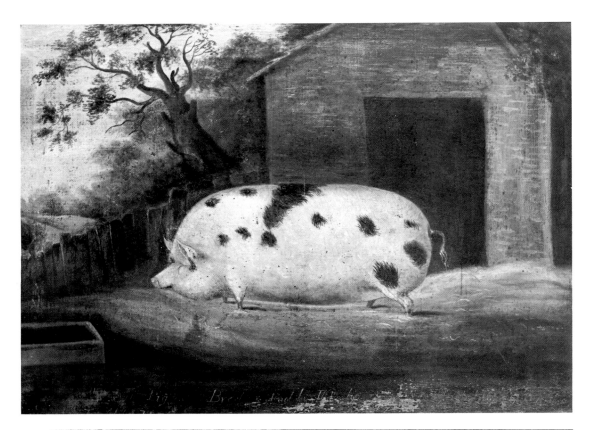

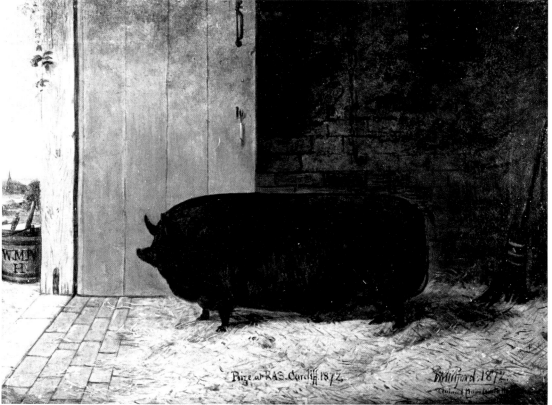

118,119 Prize pigs: top, *Gloucestershire Old Spot Pig*, by J. Miles of Northleach, Glos, 1834; above, *A Berkshire Pig: A Prize at RAS Cardiff 1872*, by Richard Whitford ('Animal Painter to the Queen'), 1872.

The sea

FOR THE VERNACULAR ARTIST seascapes, like landscapes, were seldom important in themselves but they often provided essential backgrounds for ship portraits. With a 'group portrait' a fleet (or, in battle scenes, two fleets) would be shown 'compressed', and in these circumstances the sea is all but irrelevant to the composition.

126   The painting of *Admiral Rodney defeating the French off Dominica in 1782* is an outstanding example of a vernacular marine painting. In the regularity of the waves and masts and the irregular flutter of the pennants the picture resembles a sheet of music. It could also be 'read' like a textile design which could be extended indefinitely. In this respect it is reminiscent of the much earlier and better-known painting of the Armada (1588), also by an unknown artist, which is thought to have been a design for a tapestry and is now at the National Maritime Museum, Greenwich.

As with landscapes, it was the Dutch of the seventeenth century, the Van de Veldes and others, who laid the foundation of English marine painting of the eighteenth century. English artists like Brooking and Pocock, specializing in 'sea pieces', were not above painting the less imaginative but more technical diagrams known as 'ship's likenesses' for which there was a great demand amongst captains and owners. The desire for portraits of sailing ships continued throughout the nineteenth century, but the introduction of steam driven vessels with iron hulls marked a notable decline in the demand for, and quality of, such pictures. Perhaps the men who navigated the new mechanical vessels were different, perhaps the variables of wind and sail were more picturesque.

As with animal portraits, ship portraits were commissioned by practical men who were always concerned with the subject matter but not always with the language of painting. Accordingly, artists of many levels made shipping pictures, from professional artists with academic training to downright amateurs who were or had been professional seamen. The house painters Walters of Bristol are known to have painted at least one ship portrait. Their *William Miles of Bristol* is dated 1827, and in common with so many portraits of ships (as for that matter botanical specimens) it shows the one subject from two vantage points as if two vessels were represented. Seamen, it appears, liked the prow to be visible in profile and the stern to be shown from astern, and not a few naive paintings combine both by means of distortion which is expressed with such flourish as to be almost unnoticeable. The size of ship portraits varied but in England 20 ins by 30 ins seems to have been a popular size.

The Walters family[1] were not exceptional in working both as house painters and marine artists. The late eighteenth/early nineteenth century trade label of 'Bowen and Fuss, Painters and Glaziers in General' of '29 Artichoke Lane, near Sampson's Gardens, Wapping', adds as a postscript, 'N.B. Ships Likeness's taken'.[2] Another versatile painter was the late nineteenth-century F. Tudgay of London who worked for the ship builder Richard Green at Blackwall decorating the interiors of ships. In fact the connection between ship painting and painting ships was probably very close. Edward Edwards mentions Charles Brooking (1723?–59) who 'had been bred in some department in the dock-yard at Deptford, but practiced as a ship-painter . . .' and another example cited by Edwards is John Clevely, who also trained at Deptford.[3] The great mercantile ports and the royal dockyards were populated by those who were well informed on matters of shipping. On the basis of knowledge gleaned in this way it was possible for John Ward (1798–1849), a master mariner's son who had been apprenticed to a house and ship painter, to emerge as the leading marine artist in the port of Hull. It would seem that

122

to be successful in this type of painting it was essential to have experience of the sea and ships as did William Anderson, Samuel Atkins, James Wilson Carmichael, George Chambers, William John Huggins, Thomas Luny, Nicholas Pocock and Charles S. Raleigh. All of these achieved academic respectability, but more were to remain outsiders.

Because of the nature of the subject it is not always easy to establish the country of origin of a marine painting. Many paintings of British ships are by Italians, Scandinavians and even Chinese. A painting of *The Alarm of Ipswich*,[4] signed and dated E. H. Hansen, 1856, is probably an example.[5] 130 A painting of *A foreign port* (perhaps in the East Indies) is probably by a British sailor working under foreign skies, although the depiction of Admiral Rodney's victory off Dominica is certainly English and does not suggest that the artist had any experience of the Caribbean.

127, 128, 129 Sailors' crafts (such as scrimshaw and macramé) were universal, but sailors' woolwork pictures seem to have been peculiar to Britain. Most date from the second half of the nineteenth century, and many show Royal Naval vessels, suggesting that they were not made by merchant seamen. 131, 143 The rare soldier's woolwork pictures would also point to their origin in the armed services. The few known examples which portray American vessels were probably made by English seamen such as George H. Russell, who was born in 1844 and later in life settled at the Lake Ontario village of Sacketts Harbour.[6]

In contrast to woolwork, scrimshaw (the engraving, or making of household objects from marine ivory) was common to both England and North America. Herman Melville in *Moby Dick* (1851) in his famous and lengthy description of 'skrimshandering' argues that true art is universal and timeless because it is fundamentally primitive. Thus Melville was probably the first writer to see that a naive art (scrimshaw) could be important, and perhaps the first to see ethnographic artifacts as art:

As with the Hawaiian savage, so with the white sailor-savage. With the same marvellous patience, and with the same single shark's tooth, or his one poor jack-knife, he will carve you a bit of bone sculpture, not quite as workmanlike, but as close packed in its maziness of design as the Greek savage, Achilles' shield; and full of barbaric spirit and suggestiveness as the prints of that fine old Dutch savage, Albert Durer.

Pictures without paint

WHEN THE ROYAL ACADEMY OF ARTS was established in 1769 it was determined that 'No needlework, artificial flowers, cut paper, shell work, or any such baubles should be admitted.'[1] Oil paint, bronze, marble and terracotta were the media of the Academicians, painters or sculptors, although watercolour was acceptable for preliminary studies. Other materials such as stone and wood were disdained. At the vernacular level such prejudices were unknown. Professional non-academic painters of course used oil paint on canvas, but they also employed distemper on plaster and milk-based paints on wood. Amateur artists were even more various in the materials they used and the surfaces they decorated. Butterflies, cloth, feathers, fishbones, sand, seaweed, seeds, shells, straw and, above all, embroidery and cut paper were materials employed in 'ladies' amusements'. Cut paper appeared in many guises. Amongst the earliest was the rolled paper work so popular in the eighteenth century when it was often used behind glass as the back-plate to a sconce, or framed as a picture in its own right. Feather pictures and shellwork were treated in much the same way. One of the best-known exponents of these genteel crafts was Mary Granville (1700–88), later Mrs Pendarves, best known by her name through her second marriage as Mrs Delany. Horace Walpole, in his *Anecdotes of Painting in England* (1762), credits her with the

132

147, 148

invention of 'the art of the paper mosaic, which she exerted with a precision and truth unparalleled'. These flower pictures with their black backgrounds recall her early enthusiasm for japanning.[2] She began her *Flora Delanica* in 1773 and taught the skill to Princess Elizabeth, a daughter of George III who, in recognition of her work, granted her a house and a pension.[3]

134, 135   Another ladies' pastime was the pin-pricked pictures which were particularly popular in Roman Catholic girls schools – many of the subjects are religious. The technique may have derived from the practice of pricking designs through paper so that an image could be 'pounced' onto another surface. For these pictures large areas of tone were apparently achieved by means of a toothed wheel, whilst details such as hands and faces were usually rendered in watercolour. *The Young Ladies' Book: a Manual of Elegant Recreations, Exercises, and Pursuits* recommends that '. . . the whole of the background or body of the paper [should be] painted in some sombre opaque colour to throw up the figure.'[4] Cowper's lines *On the Receipt of my Mother's Picture* could be referring to this pastime:

> Could Time, his flight reversed, restore the hours
> When, playing with thy vestures' tissued flowers,
> The violets, the pink, the jessamin,
> I prick'd them into paper with a pin.

The *Manual of Elegant Recreations* describes the activity as 'Piercing Costumes on Paper' and suggests as subject matter 'Turkish or other figures in oriental costume or draperies'.[5] 'Pin Prickt' pictures and cut paper Valentines were, like the more common silhouettes, particularly popular between the years 1810 and 1840. These examples of ladies' 'accomplishments' were originally elegantly framed by professional 'Carvers and Gilders'. A set of early nineteenth-century feather pictures in the Judkyn/Pratt Collection bear the label on the back of the original frames of J. W. Freeman of London Lane, Norwich, who advertised 'Needlework: Neatly Framed & Glazed'.

Undoubtedly of all these pastimes embroidery was the most popular and restful, though it had its dangers for that reason: 'Many hours of a woman's life are devoted to employments that do not occupy the mind, such as plain sewing, embroidery, knitting, netting, etc., and this time is generally spent in vague revery,' warned *The Young Lady's Friend*, which went on to recommend the example of 'a highly gifted lady [who] had . . . learned to divide her sight between her book and her needle . . .'[6]

Most of the products of these amateur artists were domestic in character, far removed from the still and mystic icons of Eastern Europe or the passionate *retablos* of Latin America. Although an English gentlewoman may have drawn from the scriptures for inspiration her pictures were seldom as explicitly religious as the 1834 embroidery by Elizabeth S. Gillard.

132

The fashionable 'dressed picture' of the eighteenth century became, in the course of the nineteenth century, the theatrical portrait of the kind printed by William West and others, which were 'dressed' as early as 1823 with embossed metal foil.[7] The relief picture in cloth and card by a Miss Gimbler, which is signed and dated 'AD 1865' is probably related to the earlier type of dressed picture. Such objects, like the *Butcher's Shop* (p. 54), should perhaps be considered as relief sculptures rather than pictures in the ordinary sense of the word.

136
30

It should not be assumed that because so many of these productions were the work of middle-class women of leisure none were made by men in less exalted circumstances. A two-dimensional work in the Judkyn/Pratt Collection, constructed in teak (perhaps a recycled draining-board) and inlaid with ivory (possibly old knife handles), is in the form of a 'picture' of a Victorian Gothic house called 'Newlands' set in a park. The back of this weighty object is inscribed 'DONE BY W. ROBERTS, PORTER, RUTHIN CASTLE, 1860.'

Not all those who made cloth pictures were amateurs. James Williams of Wrexham and the better-known George Smart of Tunbridge Wells were tailors by trade. Williams is known by one remarkable patchwork which he assembled between the years 1842 and 1852, and which reveals an aesthetic outlook that could have been appropriate one hundred years later. He is listed in Slater's (formerly Pigot & Co) *Royal National Commercial Directory* of 1858–9 as occupying premises in College Street, Wrexham. Less original than James Williams was George Smart, who is the subject in the following account in *Clifford's Guide to Tunbridge Wells*:

149

The company from the Wells, in their rides through Frant, are agreeably attracted on entering the village by the *nouvelle* Exhibition of a taylor, who out of cloth of divers colours, delineates animals and birds of various descriptions, with a variety of grotesque characters, particularly old Bright, the Postman, many years sweeper of Tunbridge Wells Walks, which is considered a good likeness. He has many visitors to inspect this singular collection, who seldom leave his house without becoming purchasers. He calls himself 'Artist in Cloth and Velvet Figures to His Royal Highness the Duke of Sussex', who with his characteristic good humour, patronises the humble *taylor*. He is not a little proud of his *royal* patronage, which, with the following lines [reproduced on page 149], penned by the village bard he never forgets to place at the back of his ingenious productions.[8]

Tunbridge Wells Museum possesses a fine collection of Smart's pictures and also a copy of the verse by an unknown writer:

IMPROMPTU TO THE INGENIOUS MAKER OF CLOTH AND
VELVET FIGURES OF FRANT, NR TUNBRIDGE WELLS.

Come here, I say, come here ye quizzers
Who laugh at Taylors and at scissors,
And see how *Smart* makes that utensil
Out-do the Chisel, Brush and Pencil.
With Genius Quick, and true to Nature,
He makes a suit for every creature;
And fits alike the whole creation,
In newest style the latest Fashion.
Illustrious Smart! Why stayed thou here
Like Violet in the Desert Sir?
Hide not thy modest merit thus
Nor Fame that is thy right refuse.
To the great city haste away
There give thy genius scope and play.
In Glory's circle claim thy entry,
And vie with *Lawrence, Shee,* or *Chantry.*

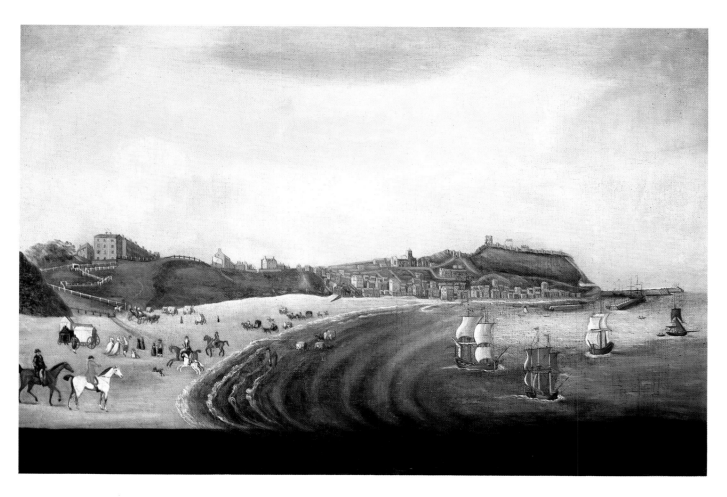

120 *Scarborough*, early nineteenth century, oil on canvas, is similar to an aquatint by W. Green after J. Hornsey's *A South View of Scarborough.*

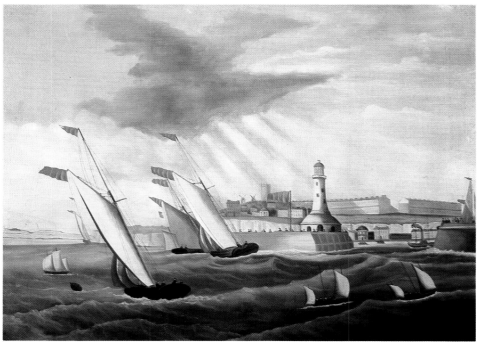

121 *A Yacht Race at Whitehaven*, 1795, oil on canvas.

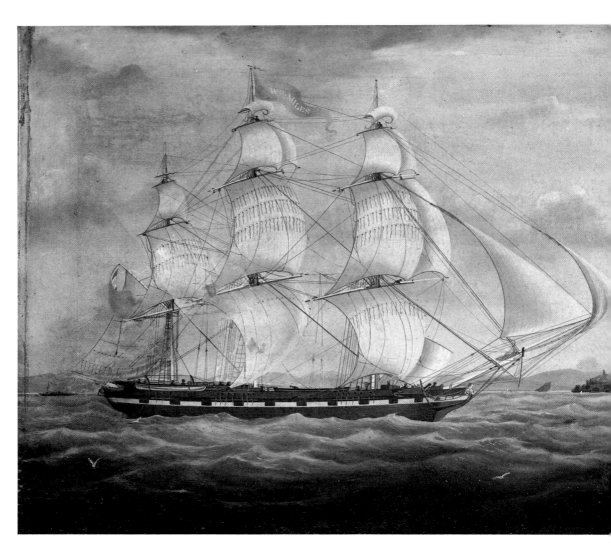

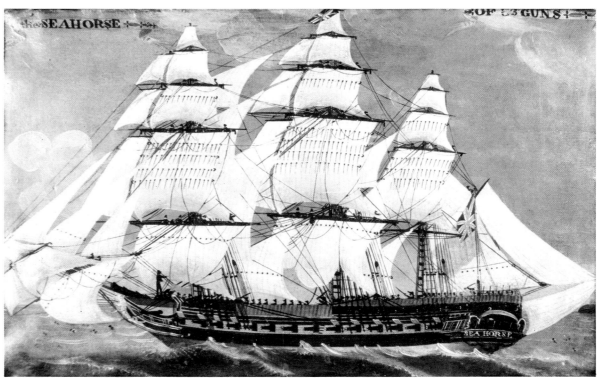

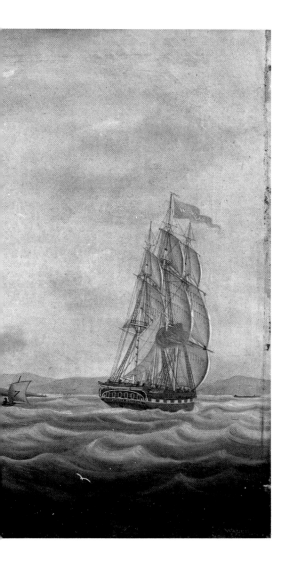

122,124 Opposite, *The 'William Miles' of Bristol*, signed 'Walters', 1827, oil on canvas. Thomas Walters was a house painter who would turn his hand to the occasional mural or easel painting. Below, *The Lowestoft Lifeboat*, by J. Starling, oil on canvas.

123 Opposite, *The Seahorse of 33 Guns*, early nineteenth century, is painted in oil on cardboard, anticipating the methods of the early twentieth-century naive artist Alfred Wallis.

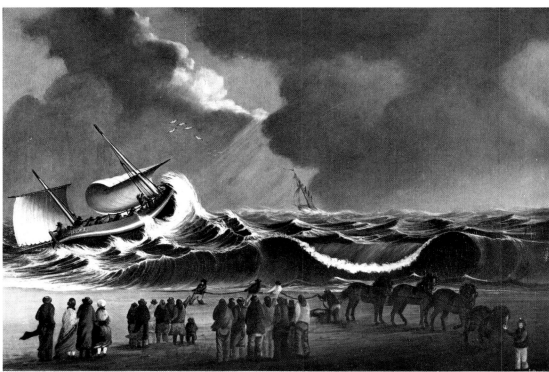

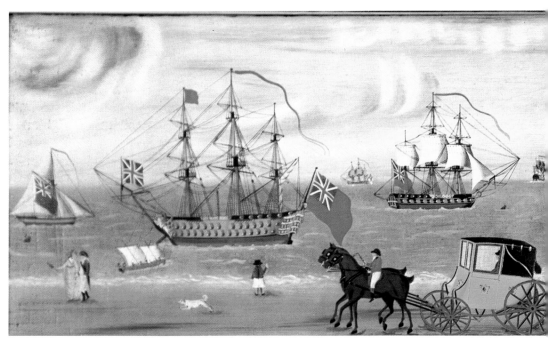

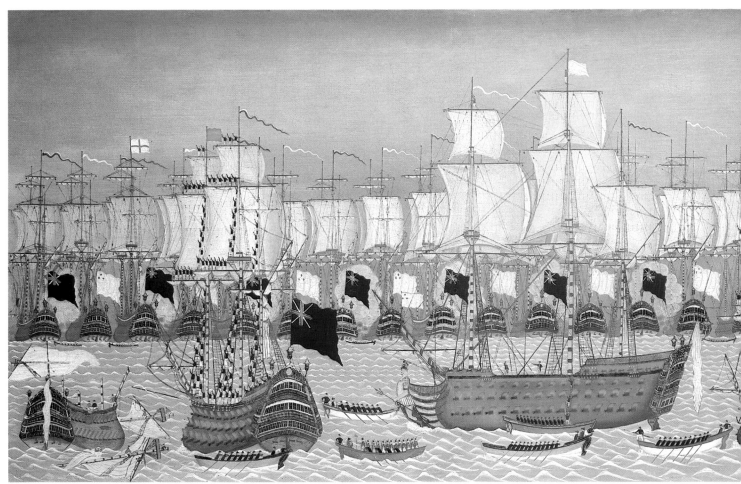

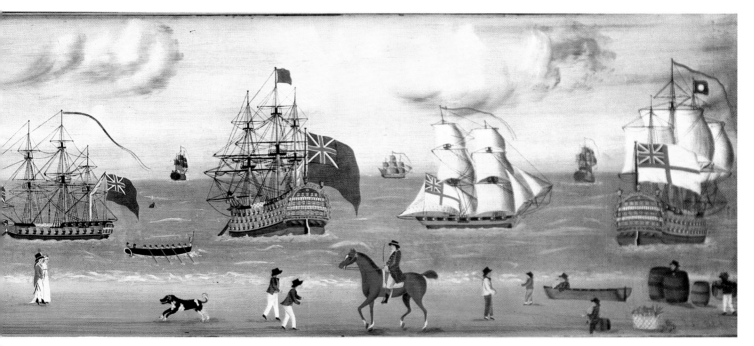

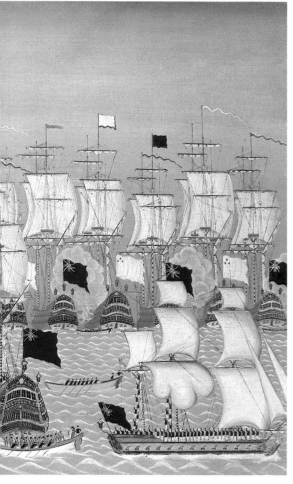

125,126 Above, *The Fleet Off-shore*, last quarter of the eighteenth century, oil on panel; left, *Admiral Rodney defeating the French fleet of 35 sail under Vice Admiral Comte de Grasse off Dominica, 12 April 1782*, oil on canvas.

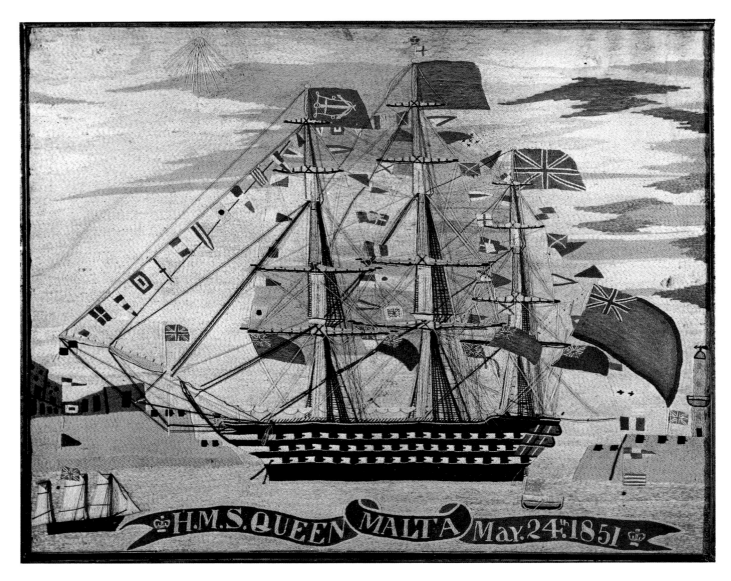

127 *HMS Queen*, Malta, 1851, woolwork
embroidery. This sailor's woolwork picture was
made to celebrate Queen Victoria's birthday,
May 24 (later Empire Day).

128,129 Opposite, Two shipping pictures in
woolwork: above, *HMS Serapis*, mid
nineteenth century, with a steam tugboat in the
left foreground; below, *Ships in an Estuary*, of
the same date.

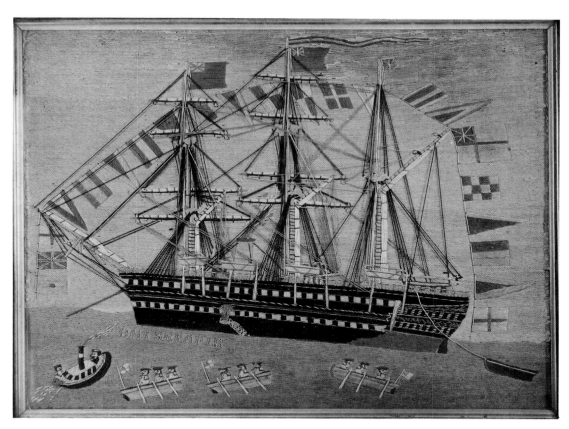

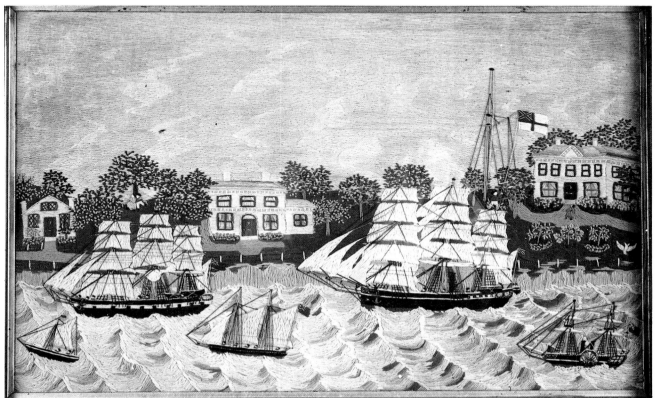

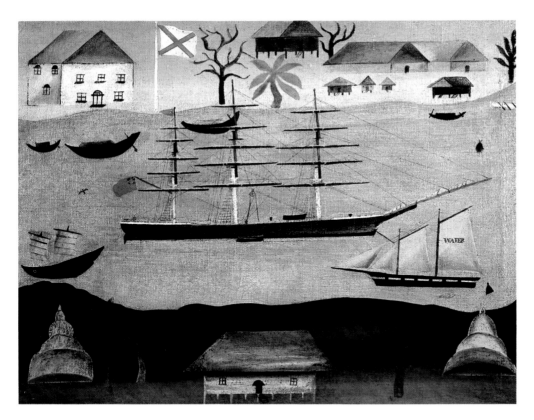

130,131 Two 'ship's likenesses':
above, *A Foreign Port*, mid
nineteenth century, oil on canvas.
The structures in the foreground
suggest Southeast Asia as a
location; right, *The Yacht
'Sunbeam' in the Solent*, a
woolwork picture made by a
soldier, Gunner G. Baldie,
c. 1850.

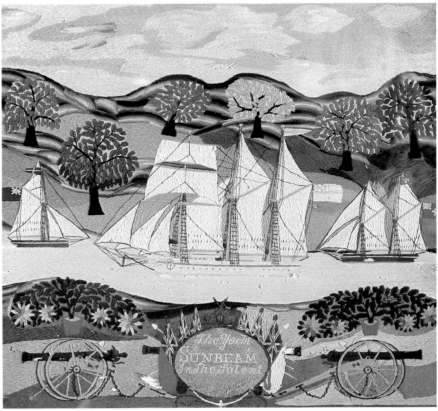

132 *Resurrection*, an embroidery
with watercolour by Elizabeth S.
Gillard, 1834, with sewn-on
features cut from engravings.
English naive art is seldom as
explicitly religious as in this
product from a genteel middle-
class background.

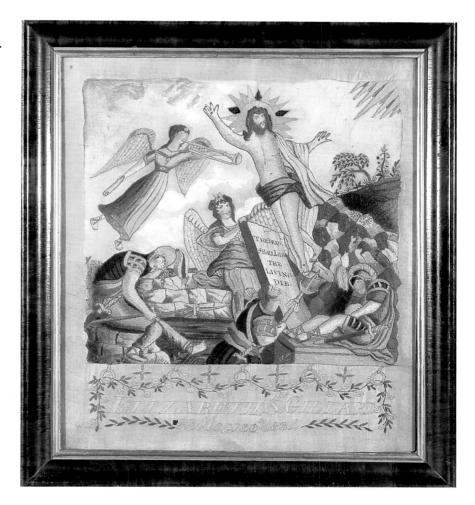

133 *Blessed are the Meek*, second
half of nineteenth century, collage
of butterflies on board with oil
paint and sand. A Wigan
newspaper found on the back of
this picture may indicate its
origin.

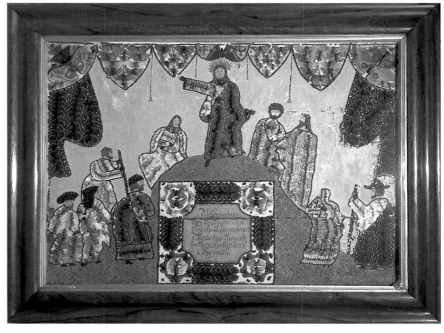

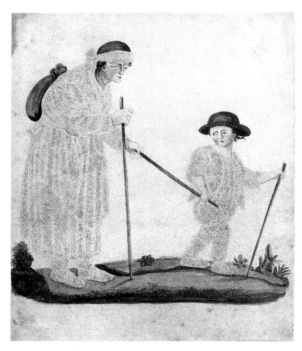

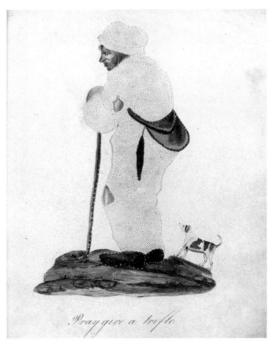

Pray give a trifle

134,135 Above, two early nineteenth-century pin-prick and watercolour pictures: *A Blind Beggar Being Led by a Child*, and *The Beggar – 'Pray Give a Trifle'*.

136 Below, *Pedestrians with a Crossing Sweeper*, by 'Miss Gimbler', 1865, feltwork relief in wood shadow box. Figures include a policeman, a soldier, and a railway guard.

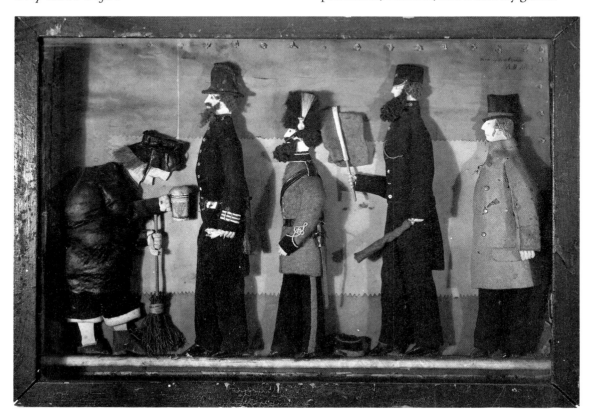

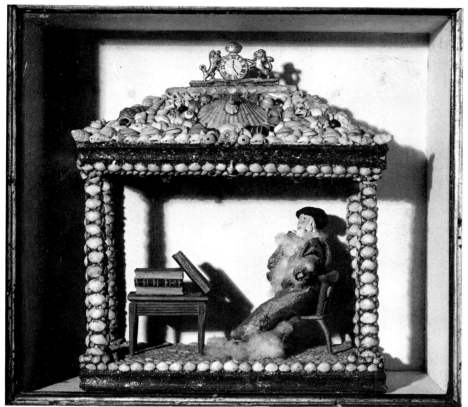

137 *Cranmer in his Study*, by
R. Brooke, 1817, wood and silk
set in a shellwork pavilion and
housed in a shadow box.
Shellwork was a popular pastime
for eighteenth-century ladies.

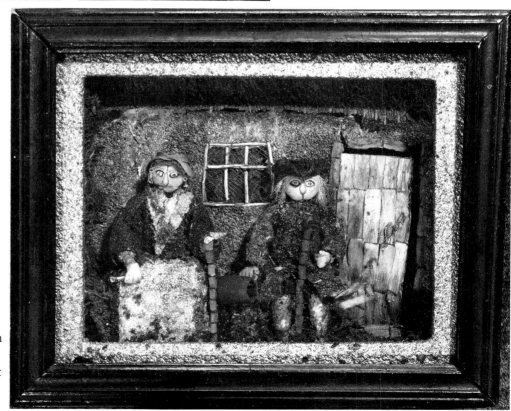

138 *An Old Man and an Old
Woman outside a House*, late
eighteenth century, seed picture in
contemporary shadow box.
Pictures were also constructed out
of fishbones, sand, seaweed and
straw.

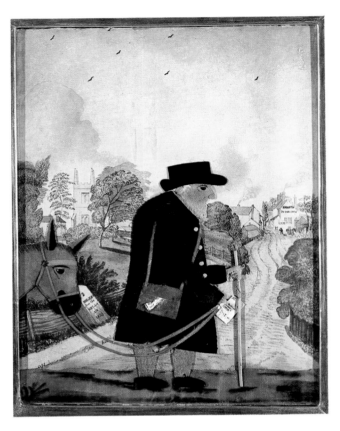

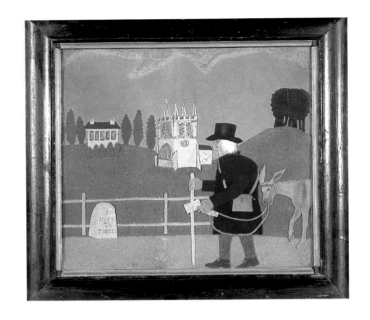

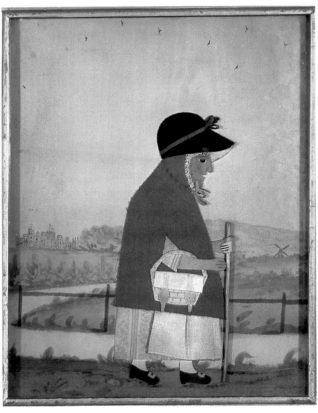

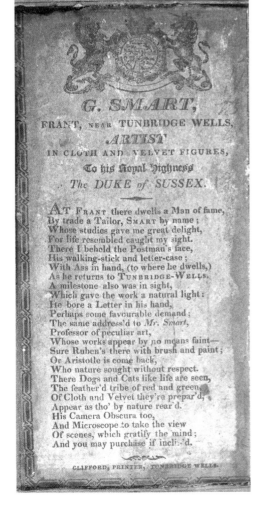

G. SMART,

FRANT, NEAR TUNBRIDGE WELLS,

ARTIST

IN CLOTH AND VELVET FIGURES,

To his Royal Highness

The DUKE of SUSSEX.

AT FRANT there dwells a Man of fame,
By trade a Tailor, SMART by name;
Whose studies gave me great delight,
For life resembled caught my sight.
There I behold the Postman's face,
His walking-stick and letter-case;
With Ass in hand, (to where he dwells,)
As he returns to TUNBRIDGE-WELLS.
A milestone also was in sight,
Which gave the work a natural light:
He bore a Letter in his hand,
Perhaps some favourable demand;
The same address'd to *Mr. Smart*,
Professor of peculiar art,
Whose works appear by no means faint—
Sure Ruben's there with brush and paint;
Or Aristotle is come back,
Who nature sought without respect.
There Dogs and Cats like life are seen,
The feather'd tribe of red and green,
Of Cloth and Velvet they're prepar'd,
Appear as tho' by nature rear'd.
His Camera Obscura too,
And Microscope to take the view
Of scenes, which gratify the mind;
And you may purchase if inclin'd.

CLIFFORD, PRINTER, TUNBRIDGE WELLS.

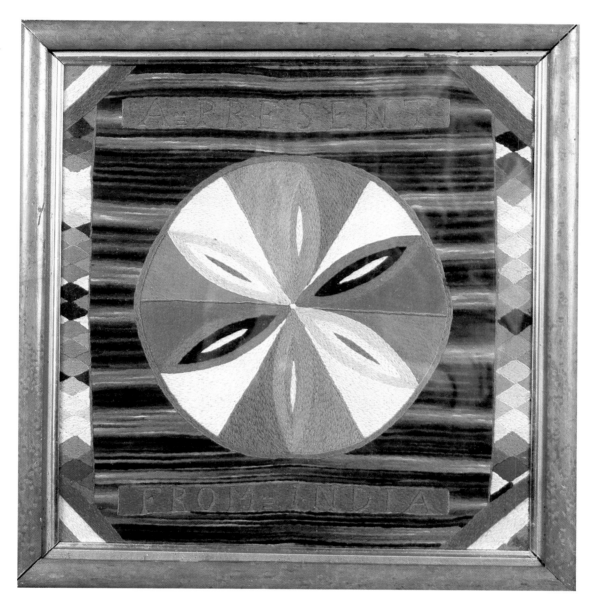

143 *A Present from India*, by 'J. Wackett 4th Battalion Rifle Brigade', mid nineteenth century, woolwork. Tantra art may have been the inspiration for this design.

139,140,141,142 Opposite, trade label and feltworks by George Smart, the famous nineteenth-century 'Taylor of Frant': above, two pictures of *Old Bright, the Postman*, with Smart's own workshop (left), and metal foil pennants for the new church tower (right). Below, *Elizabeth Horne, the Goose Woman*, c. 1830.

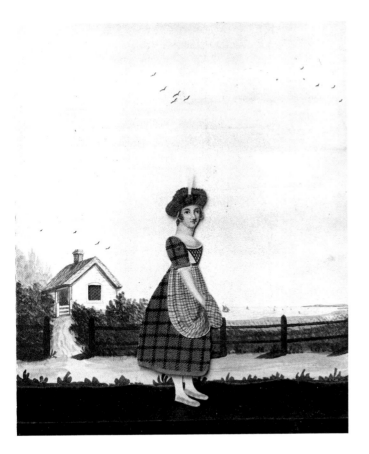

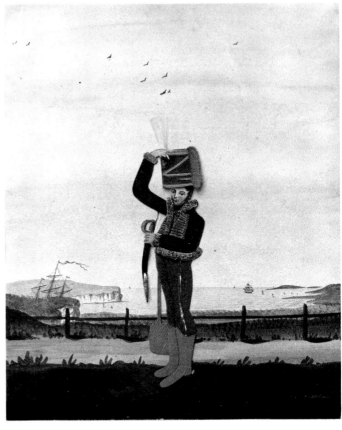

144,145 Above, early nineteenth-century feltworks by George Smart: left, *The Scottish Girl*, right, *The Hussar*. The arm is articulated so that the Hussar may doff his shako.

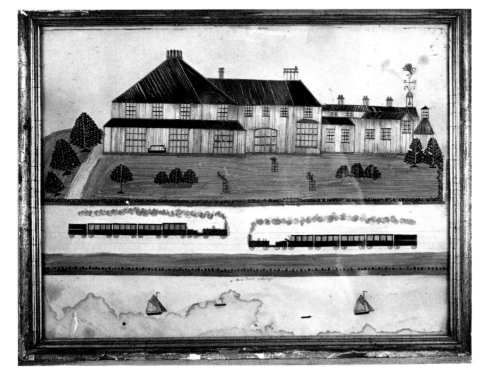

146 *Min Don, Colwyn Bay, c.* 1850, straw work and gouache on paper. One of a group of straw works depicting North Welsh scenes, all probably by the same hand. The railway helps to date the picture.

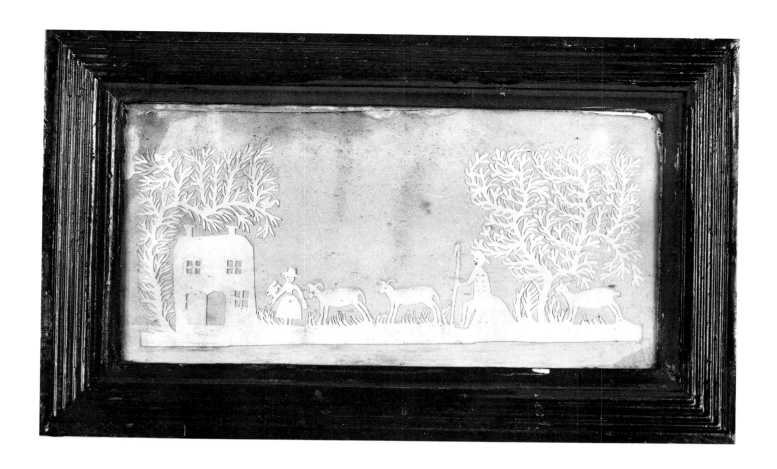

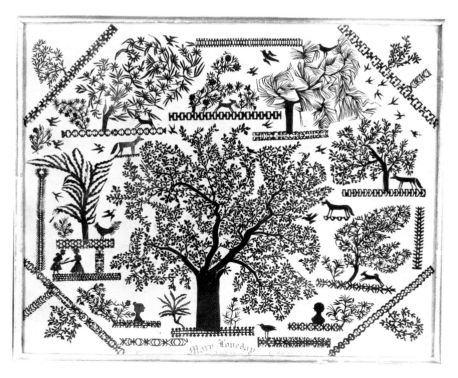

147 Above, *Goatherd with Goats*, by Mrs Jane West, 1838, cut paper. The back of the frame is inscribed, 'Cut by Mrs Jane West Apl 1838 for Elias Merrick.'

148 *Cut Paper Trees*, by Mary Loveday, 1844. The inscription reads, 'Presented by Mary Loveday Aged 68 to Miss Cleveland 1844.'

149 Overleaf, *Patchwork Bedcover*, by James Williams of Wrexham, 1842–52, pieced cloth. Williams, a tailor, used fragments of cloth from his workshop to make a composition including symbols of the British Isles, biblical scenes (Adam naming the beasts, Cain and Abel, Noah's Ark, and Jonah and the Whale), and recent engineering projects (the Menai suspension bridge, 1826, and the Ruabon viaduct, 1848). All these disparate elements are organized within a 'dazzle' pattern, producing a work far in advance of its time.

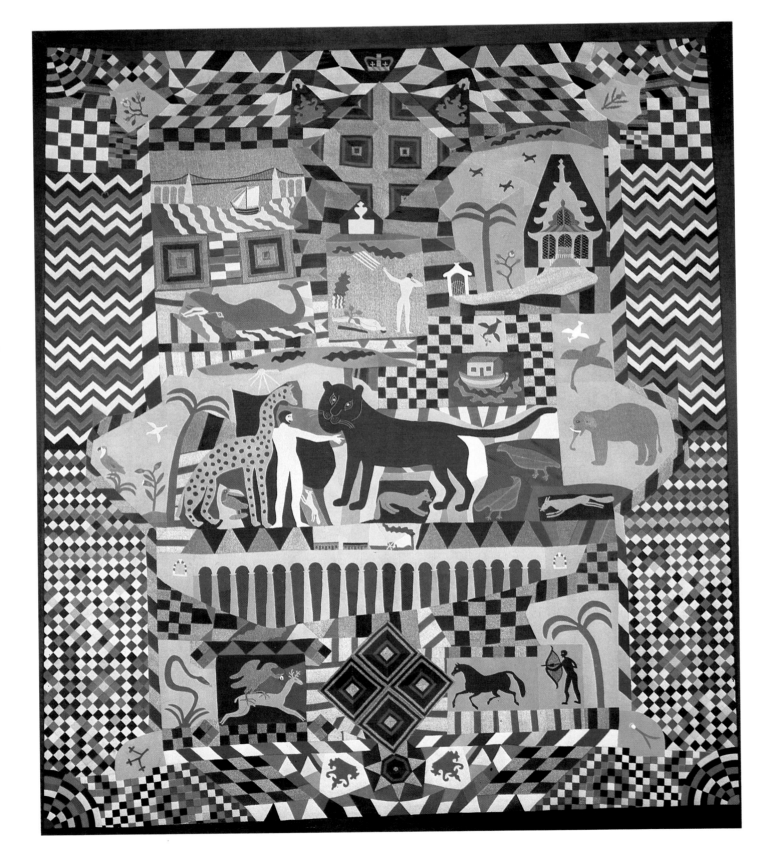

Bibliography

AYRES, JAMES *British Folk Art*, Barrie and Jenkins, London, 1976; The Overlook Press, New York, 1977

BANKS, STEVEN *The Handicrafts of the Sailor*, David and Charles, Newton Abbot, 1974

BIHALJI-MERIN, OTO *Modern Primitives*, Thames and Hudson Ltd, London, 1971

BOALCH, D. H. *Prints and Paintings of British Farm Livestock, 1780–1910*, Rothamsted Experimental Station, Hertfordshire, 1958

CARRINGTON, NOEL *Popular Art in Britain*, Penguin Books Ltd, London, 1945

EDWARDS, EDWARD *Anecdotes of the Painters*, London, 1808

EVANS, HILARY AND MARY *John Kay of Edinburgh*, Impulse Publications, Aberdeen, 1973

FLETCHER, GEOFFREY *Popular Art in England*, George G. Harrap & Co. Ltd, London, 1962

GAUNT, WILLIAM *Marine Painting*, Secker and Warburg Ltd, London, 1974

HANSEN, H. J. *European Folk Art*, Thames and Hudson Ltd, London, 1970

HANSEN, H. J. (ed.) *Art and the Seafarer*, Faber and Faber, London, 1968

JONES, BARBARA *The Unsophisticated Arts*, Architectural Press, London, 1951

LAMBERT, MARGARET, AND MARX, ENID *English Popular Art*, Batsford, London, 1951

LARWOOD, JACOB, AND HOTTEN, JOHN CAMDEN *The History of Signboards*, London, 1866

LISTER, ERIC, AND WILLIAMS, SHELDON *Twentieth Century British Naive and Primitive Artists*, Astragal Books, London, 1977

MOORE, PATRICIA AND DONALD 'A Vanished House – Two Topographical Paintings of the Old House at Margam, Glamorgan', in *Archaeologia Cambrensis*, vol. CXXIII, 1974

MULLINS, EDWIN *Alfred Wallis, Cornish Primitive Painter*, Macdonald, London, 1967

PARKIN, MICHAEL *Eight Views of Old Chelsea by Henry and Walter Greaves*, W. H. Newson Holding Ltd, London, 1975.

153

Chapter references

INTRODUCTION

1 Kenneth Ames, Catalogue Introduction, *Beyond Necessity – Art in the Folk Tradition*, Henry Francis du Pont Museum exhibition at Brandywine River Museum, Pennsylvania, 1977.

2 Henry Glassie, *Patterns in the Material Folk Culture of the Eastern United States*, University of Pennsylvania Press, 1968, p.29.

3 John Stalker and George Parker, *A Treatise of Japaning and Varnishing*, Oxford, 1688, Tiranti reprint, London, 1971, Preface.

4 J. C. Loudon, *Encyclopaedia of Cottage, Farm and Villa Architecture*, London, 1836, 1842 edition, p.352.

5 Advertisement in Morris's *Directory of Bristol*, 1872.

6 Michael Parkin, *Eight Views of Old Chelsea by Henry and Walter Greaves*, W. H. Newson Holding Ltd in association with the Parkin Gallery, London, 1975.

7 Eric Lister and Sheldon Williams, *Twentieth Century British Naive and Primitive Artists*, Astragal Books, London, 1977.

8 Oto Bihalji-Merin, *Modern Primitives*, Thames and Hudson, London, 1971, p.278.

9 *Ibid*, p.277.

10 See Herbert W. Hemphill Jr and Julia Weissman, *Twentieth Century American Folk Art and Artists*, Dutton, New York, 1974.

11 The word is however often found with its original meaning in the nineteenth century: '*Painting in watercolours* is often called *limning*.' Mrs Phelps, *The Female Student*, London, 1836.

12 Everyman's Library, Dent, London, 1908, 1917 edition, pp.84–6.

13 I am indebted to Bristol City Art Gallery for this listing.

14 Lot 176 in Christie's sale of 27 January 1978 was a painting of a *Prospect of Ilfracombe*, signed and dated John Walters, 1752, and possibly a member of the same family. I am indebted to Mr Francis Greenacre of Bristol City Art Gallery for this information.

15 See James Ayres, *The Shell Book of the Home in Britain 1500–1850: Decoration, Design and Construction of Vernacular Interiors*, Faber and Faber, London, publication announced.

16 Drake's painting was commissioned by William Tufnell of Nun Monkton Priory, Yorkshire. It was shown (no. 39) at the exhibition of *British Sporting Painting 1650–1850* at the Hayward Gallery, London, 1974.

17 Martin Hardie, *Watercolour Painting in Britain*, Batsford, London, 1968, vol. III, 'The Victorian Period', p.250.

18 British Library MS. 15513.f.6. It measures 45.7 cm × 30.5 cm (18 ins × 12 ins).

19 Sir Herbert Maxwell, *Edinburgh: A Historical Study*, Williams and Norgate, London, 1916.

20 His books, most of which were published under the pen-name of Tim Bobbin, include a number of works of local history, folklore and dialect. The plates reproduced here (Nos. 5 and 6) are based on Episodes 6 and 8 from *Human Passions Delineated* (1772–73), his remarkable book of engravings with accompanying verses. A note on the title page reads:

> NB Gentlemen etc. may have any Plate or Plates, Painted on Canvas or Pasteboard as large as the life, from 5s to 15s a Head by sending their Orders to the Author, near Rochdale.

The verse description of the first scene (Pl. 5) is as follows:

> He miss'd at first, but try'd again,
>> Then clapp'd his foot o' th' chin;
> He pull'd – the patient roar'd with pain
>> And hideously did grin . . .

The second (Pl. 6) tells the sequel:

> Now string's put fast on tooth that aches,
>> Which round his hand he wraps,
> A glowing coal i' th' tongs he takes,
>> And to his nose he claps.
> The sight and smell of fire drove back
>> The patient's head in a fright,
> Who drew his own tooth in a crack,
>> And prov'd the Doctor right.

21 Richard Townley, *The Miscellaneous Works of Tim Bobbin (with) a Life of the Author*, London, 1806, 1818 edition, p.IX.

22 J. T. Smith, *Nollekens and His Times*, London, 1829, 1919 edition, vol. I, pp.23-5.

23 Jacob Larwood and John Camden Hotten, *The History of Signboards*, London, 1866, pp.37-40.

24 Early eighteenth-century trade label in the Ambrose Heal Collection, Department of Prints and Drawings, British Museum, 90.92.

25 Larwood and Hotten, *op. cit.*, p.39.

26 Robert Dossie, *The Handmaid to the Arts*, London, 1758, 1764 edition, vol. I, ch. II, section II.

27 See 'Professors and Teachers' in Pigot's *National Commercial Directory* for Bristol of 1830.

28 By 'Mrs Phelps, late Vice-Principal of Troy Female Seminary'. The American edition came out in Boston in 1833.

29 Stalker and Parker, *op. cit.*, p.70.

30 Quoted in Larwood and Hotten, *op. cit.*, p.521.

31 *St James's Chronicle*, Tuesday 23 March 1762.

32 From 1811 to 1816 Kay exhibited each year with the Edinburgh Associated Artists and in 1822 in the fourth exhibition of *The Institute for the Encouragement of the Arts in Scotland*.

33 Fernande Olivier (Picasso's wife), quoted by Oto Bihalji-Merin, *op. cit.*, p.59.

34 See Edwin Mullins, *Alfred Wallis, Cornish Primitive Painter*, Macdonald, London, 1967, p.109.

35 *Ibid.*

PORTRAITS OF THE PEOPLE

1 William L. Sachse, *The Colonial American in Britain*, U. of Wisconsin Press, Madison Wis., 1956, p.171.

2 Chambers was known for marine views, landscapes and portraits. See *101 Masterpieces of American Painting*, American Federation of Arts, New York City, 1961, which also mentions Cowan (who was born in Scotland). For Cowan see also Nina Fletcher Little, *American Decorative Wall Painting, 1700–1850*, Dutton, New York, 1972 ed.

3 Nina Fletcher Little, *op. cit.*, p.37.

4 Richard Townley, *The Miscellaneous Works of Tim Bobbin, etc.* London, 1806, p.IX.

5 Edward Edwards, *Anecdotes of the Painters*, London, 1808, p.31.

6 Mrs Phelps, *The Female Student*, London ed., 1836.

7 I am indebted to Miss Jane Evans of Woodspring Museum, Weston-super-Mare, for showing me this collection of paintings by Sheppard as well as the certificates and other documents connected with his life.

8 Portrait of *Colour Sergeant Dollery of the 34th Cumberland Regiment, and his Family*, 1826. Courtesy of The Border Regiment and King's Own Royal Border Regiment Museum, Carlisle Castle.

TOWN LIFE

1 George Eliot, writing of the period *c.* 1832 in *Felix Holt the Radical*, 1867, Ch. I.

2 G. F. Chadwick, 'The Face of the Industrial City', in H. J. Dyos and Michael Wolff (ed.), *The Victorian City – Images and Reality*, Routledge & Kegan Paul, London, 1973 (2 vols), vol. I, pp.247-8.

3 Christopher Morris (ed.), *The Journeys of Celia Fiennes*, Cresset Press, London, 1947, p.238.

4 For reference to inn signs painted on stagecoach doors see Anthony Bird, *Roads and Vehicles*, Longman, London, 1969, Arrow Books ed., 1973, p.122.

5 See *Catchpenny Prints, 163 Popular Engravings from the Eighteenth Century*, originally published by Bowles and Carver, Dover reprint, New York, 1970, p.123.

6 William Blake, *Jerusalem 43:54*.

SPORTS AND PASTIMES

1 Joseph Strutt, *The Sports and Pastimes of the People of England*, London, 1801, 1898 edition, Introduction.

2 Edward Edwards, *Anecdotes of the Painters*, London, 1808, p.11.

3 Strutt, *op. cit.*, p.106.

4 *Pills to Purge Melancholy*, 4th edition, 1719, vol. II, p.53.

5 Introduction to the catalogue of *British Sporting Painting, 1650–1850*, Arts Council exhibition at the Hayward Gallery, London, 1974, p.11.

6 See *Chambers's Encyclopaedia*, London, 1861. The Kalman Collection includes a fine painting of 'Tom Sayers, Prize Fighter'.

7 In *Ely Gossip* (1891) Harvey Godwin (Bishop of Carlisle and previously Dean of Ely) refers to Southby, who was Verger at the Cathedral for sixty years:

> When I became Dean [in 1858] ... the lower portion on the South side [of Ely Porta] was used as a brewery. Dean and Chapter ale and small-beer were brewed by William Southby, for many years a Verger, and in other respects a

faithful servant of the Cathedral. Southby's brewings had a high reputation, especially the ale which was prepared for the great dinners given by the Dean and Chapter at the two great gatherings, Chapter and Audit. I found however that private brewing was getting a little out of date and that a post-card to Burton-on-Trent would save a great deal of dirt about the College, and would relieve Southby of work which was growing irksome. Accordingly I suggested to the Chapter that we should give up brewing . . .

8 See Michael Parkin, *Eight Views of Old Chelsea by Henry and Walter Greaves*, W. H. Newson Holding Ltd in association with the Parkin Gallery, London, 1975, which not only illustrates their topographical work but also contains useful information on the Greaves family.

RURAL LIFE

1 Phyllis Deane and W. A. Cole, *British Economic Growth, 1688–1959, Trends and Structure*, Cambridge University Press, 2nd edition, 1969, pp.99, 104.

2 Batty Langley, *The Builder's and Workman's Treasury of Designs, etc.*, 1750, contains no less than twenty designs incorporating 'Tabernacle Frames'.

3 For a brief account of artists of this type see Patricia and Donald Moore, 'A Vanished House – Two Topographical Paintings of the Old House at Margam, Glamorgan',

Archaeologia Cambrensis, vol. CXXIII, 1974.

4 Edward Edwards, *Anecdotes of the Painters*, London, 1808, pp.26–7.

5 Christopher Morris (ed.), *The Journeys of Celia Fiennes*, Cresset Press, London, 1947, p.131.

6 Anthony Bird, *Roads and Vehicles*, Longman, London, 1969, Arrow Books edition, 1973, p.122.

BIRDS AND BEASTS

1 Christopher Morris (ed.), *The Journeys of Celia Fiennes*, Cresset Press, London, 1947, p.84.

2 Thomas Bewick in his *Memoir*, Newcastle upon Tyne and London, 1862, pp.183–4.

3 D. H. Boalch, *Prints and Paintings of British Farm Livestock, 1780–1910*, Rothamsted Experimental Station, Hertfordshire, 1958, p.xvii.

4 *Ibid.*

THE SEA

1 It is not known if they were related to the well-known Samuel Walters of Liverpool (1811–1882) or to Joseph Walter of Bristol (1783–1856).

2 Ambrose Heal Collection 90.15, Department of Prints and Drawings, British Museum.

3 Edward Edwards, *Anecdotes of the Painters*, London, 1808.

4 Ipswich Museums.

5 Perhaps related to B. H. Hansen (*fl.* 1827–46) and H. C. Hansen

(*fl.* 1837—47), both of Altona, Schleswig-Holstein, which until 1864 came under the Danish crown. See Hans Jurgen Hansen (ed.), *Art and the Seafarer*, Faber and Faber, London, 1968, p.184.

6 Jonathan Fairbanks, 'The Yarns of a Sailor in Yarn', in the magazine *Antiques*, New York, September 1929.

PICTURES WITHOUT PAINT

1 Robert C. Alberts, *Benjamin West, A Biography*, Houghton Mifflin, Boston, 1978, p.96.

2 The Department of Prints and Drawings in the British Museum has a fine collection of Mrs Delany's paper mosaics.

3 Lady Llanover (ed.), *The Autobiography and Correspondence of Mary Granville, Mrs Delany*, London, 1861.

4 Quoted in E. D. Longman and S. Loch, *Pins and Pincushions*, Longman, London, 1911. Pin-pricked pictures were almost unknown in America, but the Abby Aldrich Rockefeller Folk Art Gallery does include a rare example of this work – its subject is *The Figure of Liberty*.

5 Longman and Loch, *op. cit.*

6 *The Young Lady's Friend*, 4th edition, London, 1841, pp.18, 19.

7 George Speaight, *The History of the English Toy Theatre*, Studio Vista, London, 1969, p.129.

8 Tunbridge Wells, 1822, with later editions up to 1851.

List of illustrations

Mid nineteenth century
Watercolour on paper
21.5 cm × 33.5 cm
    ($8\frac{1}{2}$ ins × $13\frac{1}{4}$ ins)
Judkyn/Pratt

17   *Profile Portrait of a Fat Boy*
     Artist unknown
     Second quarter of the
         nineteenth century
     Watercolour on paper
     34.5 cm × 23.5 cm
         ($13\frac{1}{2}$ ins × $9\frac{1}{4}$ ins)
     Judkyn/Pratt

18   *A Child with a Cat*
     Artist unknown
     Early nineteenth century
     Watercolour on paper
     15 cm × 13.5 cm
         (6 ins × $5\frac{1}{4}$ ins)
     Judkyn/Pratt

19   *A Child with a Lamb*
     Artist unknown
     First quarter of the nineteenth
         century
     Oil on panel
     58.5 cm × 42 cm
         (23 ins × $16\frac{1}{2}$ ins)
     Mr and Mrs Michael Reeves

20   *A Child with a Coral*
     Artist unknown
     Second quarter of the
         nineteenth century
     Oil on canvas
     42 cm × 56 cm
         ($16\frac{1}{2}$ ins × 22 ins)
     Mr and Mrs Michael Reeves

21   *Alfred Openshaw, Age One
         Year*
     R. Hunt
     July 1846
     Oil on canvas
     85 cm × 68 cm
         ($33\frac{1}{2}$ ins × $26\frac{3}{4}$ ins)
     Judkyn/Pratt

22   *Portrait of a Gentleman* (one of
         a set)
     Artist unknown
     1780–1800
     Gouache on paper

19 cm × 15 cm
    ($7\frac{1}{2}$ ins × 6 ins)
Judkyn/Pratt

23   *Profile Portrait of a Young
         Woman Holding a Fan*
     (as 22)

24   *Profile Portrait of a Gentleman*
     (as 22)

25   *Profile Portrait of an Old Lady
         Holding a Fan* (as 22)

26   *John Brown aged 9 years*
     Artist unknown
     'The 9 of Febary, 1855'
     Watercolour on paper
     15 cm × 13 cm
         (6 ins × 5 ins)
     Judkyn/Pratt

27   *Profile of an Old Lady
         Taking Snuff*
     Artist unknown
     Mid nineteenth century
     Watercolour on paper
     15 cm × 13 cm
         (6 ins × 5 ins)
     Judkyn/Pratt

28   *Portrait of Miss Bisdee*
     Joseph Sheppard (1834–1928)
     c. 1866–70
     Oil on canvas
     34.5 cm × 26 cm
         ($13\frac{1}{2}$ ins × $10\frac{1}{4}$ ins)
     Woodspring Museum,
         Weston-super-Mare

TOWN LIFE

29   *The Market Cross, Ipswich*
     Artist unknown
     Early nineteenth century
     Oil on board
     44.5 cm × 63.5 cm
         ($17\frac{1}{2}$ ins × 25 ins)
     Rutland Gallery, London

30   *Model Butcher's Shop*
     Artist unknown
     1875–90
     Carved wood, painted; in
         original cross-banded

mahogany shadow box
39.5 cm × 60 cm
    ($15\frac{3}{4}$ ins × $23\frac{3}{4}$ ins)
Judkyn/Pratt

31   *The Kings Arms, Manchester*
     Artist unknown
     c. 1830
     Oil on canvas
     48 cm × 75 cm
         (19 ins × $29\frac{1}{2}$ ins)
     Mr and Mrs Andras Kalman

32   *The Royal Rat Catcher*
     J. Clark
     Early nineteenth century
     Oil on canvas
     33.5 cm × 61.5 cm
         ($13\frac{1}{4}$ ins × $24\frac{1}{4}$ ins)
     Mr and Mrs Andras Kalman

33   *A View, at New Brentford,
         Middlesex*
     H. Sexton
     1804
     Watercolour on paper
     24.5 cm × 41.5 cm
         ($9\frac{3}{4}$ ins × $16\frac{1}{2}$ ins)
     Judkyn/Pratt

34   *The Eagle* or *Lady of the Lake
         Inn*
     Artist unknown
     1857
     Oil on canvas
     86.5 cm × 96.5 cm
         (34 ins × 38 ins)
     Mr and Mrs Andras Kalman

34a Recent photograph of
         The Eagle

35   *The High Street, Staines*
     Artist unknown
     Early nineteenth century
     Oil on canvas
     45.5 cm × 61 cm
         (18 ins × 24 ins)
     Photograph Rutland Gallery,
         London

36   *A Bird's Eye View of Market
         Street, Wymondham*
     Artist unknown
     c. 1850

Oil on canvas
59.7 cm × 43.2 cm
(23½ ins × 17 ins)
Rutland Gallery, London

37 *Wakefield, Old Church Steps at
    the Entrance to Teal Street*
    C. H. Hepworth
    1852
    Oil on board
    59.7 cm × 82.5 cm
    (23½ ins × 32½ ins)
    Mr and Mrs Andras Kalman

38 *A Yorkshire Street Corner*
    T. Wainwright
    1892
    Oil on canvas
    25 cm × 40.5 cm
    (9¾ ins × 16 ins)
    Mr and Mrs Andras Kalman

39 *A. Marshall, Dyer and Scourer*
    Arthur Godwin
    1908
    Oil on canvas
    59.5 cm × 90 cm
    (23½ ins × 35½ ins)
    Mr and Mrs Andras Kalman

40 *The Public Baths, Coventry*
    W. E. Reeve
    1873
    Oil on panel
    39.5 cm × 58.5 cm
    (15½ ins × 23 ins)
    Herbert Art Gallery and
    Museum, Coventry

41 *The Park, Coventry*
    Herbert Rylance
    c. 1885
    Oil on panel
    46.5 cm × 63 cm
    (18½ ins × 23¾ ins)
    Herbert Art Gallery and
    Museum, Coventry

42 *All Saints Church, Northampton*
    Artist unknown
    c. 1830–35
    Oil on canvas
    91.5 cm × 120 cm
    (36 ins × 47 ins)

Central Museum and Art
Gallery, Northampton

43 *Broad Quay, Bristol*
    Artist unknown
    First half of the eighteenth
    century
    Oil on canvas
    64 cm × 78 cm
    (25¼ ins × 30¾ ins)
    City of Bristol, Museums and
    Art Gallery

44 *An Election Meeting, Blackburn
    Market Place, 1832*
    Artist unknown
    c. 1832
    Oil on canvas
    54 cm × 65 cm
    (21½ ins × 25½ ins)
    Blackburn Museum and Art
    Gallery

45 *A View of Bristol*
    J. Marshall
    1880
    Oil on canvas
    48.9 cm × 58.4 cm
    (19 ins × 23 ins)
    Rutland Gallery, London

46 *A Riverside View of London*
    Artist unknown
    c. 1840–50
    Oil on canvas
    228.5 cm × 61 cm
    (90 ins × 24 ins)
    Dr and Mrs Milan Sladek

47 *Black Street Sweeper*
    B. Sturr
    c. 1850
    Oil on canvas
    40 cm × 50 cm
    (15¾ ins × 19¾ ins)
    Mr and Mrs Andras Kalman

48 *Waiting outside Number 12*
    Artist unknown
    c. 1850
    Oil on canvas
    59 cm × 85.5 cm
    (23¼ ins × 33¾ ins)
    Mr and Mrs Andras Kalman

SPORTS AND PASTIMES

49 *Hare and Hounds*
    Artist unknown
    c. 1840
    Painted tin tray
    45.7 cm × 60.9 cm
    (18 ins × 24 ins)
    Mr and Mrs Andras Kalman

50 *Pheasant Shooting*
    Artist unknown
    c. 1840
    Painted tin tray
    39.5 cm × 56 cm
    (15½ ins × 22 ins)
    Mr and Mrs James Ayres

51 A fourfold screen divided into
    eight panels
    Artist unknown
    'Marc y 31st 1746'
    Oil on canvas
    198 cm × 282 cm
    (78 ins × 111 ins)
    Victoria and Albert Museum,
    London

52 *The Hunt*
    Artist unknown
    c. 1850
    Watercolour on paper
    44 cm × 62 cm
    (17½ ins × 24½ ins)
    Judkyn/Pratt

53 *A Difficult Fence*
    J. Baker
    Late eighteenth century
    Oil on canvas
    38 cm × 75.5 cm
    (15 ins × 29¾ ins)
    Photograph Rutland Gallery,
    London

54 *A Hunt in Full Cry*
    William Meagher
    'Aug 23rd 1745'
    Oil on canvas
    86.5 cm × 107 cm
    (34 ins × 42 ins)
    Private collection

55 *The Cricket Match*
Attributed to W. R. Coates
c. 1750
Oil on canvas
49 cm × 59 cm
  (19¼ ins × 23¼ ins)
Tate Gallery, London

56 *Boy with Kite*
Artist unknown
c. 1870
Oil on cardboard
28 cm × 23 cm
  (11 ins × 9 ins)
Mr and Mrs Andras Kalman

57 *Boy with Cricket Bat*
Artist unknown
c. 1870
Oil on cardboard
28 cm × 23 cm
  (11 ins × 9 ins)
Mr and Mrs Andras Kalman

58 *The Stag Hunt*
Artist unknown
1781
Oil on canvas
77.5 cm × 161.5 cm
  (30½ ins × 63¾ ins)
Colonial Williamsburg
  Foundation

59 *A Huntsman with Hounds*
Artist unknown
Mid nineteenth century
Oil on canvas
66 cm × 94 cm
  (26 ins × 37 ins)
Photograph Rutland Gallery,
  London

60 *The Poacher*
Artist unknown
Early nineteenth century
Oil on panel
31.7 cm × 26 cm
  (12½ ins × 10¼ ins)
Mr and Mrs Andras Kalman

61 *Hammersmith Bridge on Boat
  Race Day*
Walter Greaves (1846–1930)
c. 1862

Oil on canvas
91.5 cm × 140 cm
  (36 ins × 55 ins)
Tate Gallery, London

62 *Thames Nocturne*
Walter Greaves (1846–1930)
Third quarter of the
  nineteenth century
Oil on canvas
33.5 cm × 50 cm
  (13 ins × 19½ ins)
Hunterian Museum,
  University of Glasgow

63 *Ely Cathedral: Luncheon in
  Dean's Pasture on the occasion
  of the marriage of Princess
  Alexandra to Prince Albert
  Edward, 1863*
J. W. H. Southby (1801–80)
1863
Oil on canvas
35.5 cm × 40.5 cm
  (14 ins × 16 ins)
Dean and Chapter, Ely
  Cathedral

64 *The Race Course*
Artist unknown
Mid nineteenth century
Oil on canvas
30.5 cm × 147.3 cm
  (12 ins × 58 ins)
Rutland Gallery, London.

65 *A Race Horse with the Jockey up*
Artist unknown
Late eighteenth century
Oil on board
30 cm × 40.5 cm
  (11¾ ins × 16 ins)
Mr and Mrs Andras Kalman

66 *The Winner's Enclosure*
Artist unknown
Mid nineteenth century
Oil on canvas
41.9 cm × 52.7 cm
  (16½ ins × 20½ ins)
Mr and Mrs Andras Kalman

67 *Irish Fighting Cocks*
R. Brown
1872
Oil on board
42 cm × 53.5 cm
  (16½ ins × 21 ins)
Mr and Mrs Andras Kalman

68 *Nell, the Rat-hunter*
J. Whitehead
1852
Oil on canvas
51.5 cm × 65 cm
  (20½ ins × 25½ ins)
Mr and Mrs Andras Kalman

69 *The Rat Pit*
Artist unknown
c. 1855
Oil on board
24 cm × 29 cm
  (9½ ins × 11½ ins)
Mr and Mrs Andras Kalman

70 *Bear Baiting*
Artist unknown
Mid nineteenth century
Oil on canvas
29.2 cm × 34.3 cm
  (11½ ins × 13½ ins)
Mr and Mrs Andras Kalman

71 *The West Bromwich Sweep*
Artist unknown
c. 1850
Watercolour on paper
50.5 cm × 39.5 cm
  (20 ins × 15½ ins)
Mr and Mrs Andras Kalman

RURAL LIFE

72 *Still Life with Cheshire Cheese*
John Booth Higginson
1869
Oil on canvas
63 cm × 75 cm
  (24½ ins × 29½ ins)
Judkyn/Pratt

73 *Fallen Greatness*
Mary Merrall
1880

Oil on canvas
50.8 cm × 76.2 cm
(20 ins × 30 ins)
Photograph Rutland Gallery,
London

74 *Midsummer Night's Dream*
W. Balls
c. 1860
Oil on canvas
51 cm × 63.5 cm
(20 ins × 25 ins)
Mr and Mrs Andras Kalman

75 *A Shepherd with an English
Sheep Dog*
Artist unknown
c. 1820
Oil on canvas
94 cm × 78.5 cm
(37 ins × 31 ins)
Mr and Mrs Derek Balmer

76 *A Country Schoolroom*
Artist unknown
c. 1850
Oil on canvas
53.3 cm × 83.8 cm
(21 ins × 33 ins)
Photograph Rutland Gallery,
London

77 *A Village Street*
Artist unknown
c. 1840
Oil on canvas
63.5 cm × 76 cm
(25 ins × 30 ins)
Photograph Rutland Gallery,
London

78 *Bringing Home the Cows*
Artist unknown
Late eighteenth century
Oil on canvas
67 cm × 90 cm
(26½ ins × 35½ ins)
Mr and Mrs Andras Kalman

79 *Nine Angry Bulls*
Artist unknown
Mid nineteenth century
Oil on canvas

49.5 cm × 73.6 cm
(19½ ins × 29 ins)
Mr and Mrs Andras Kalman

80 *At the Magpie Inn*
John Cordrey
Early nineteenth century
Oil on board
20 cm × 25 cm
(8 ins × 10 ins)
Photograph Rutland Gallery,
London

81 *Landscape with Exotic Buildings*
Artist unknown
Mid eighteenth century
Oil on canvas
91.5 cm × 132 cm
(36 ins × 52 ins)
Mr Roger Bichard

82 *Village Scene*
Artist unknown
Late nineteenth century
Oil on cardboard
15 cm × 21.5 cm
(6 ins × 8½ ins)
Mr Roger Bichard

83 *Village Scene*
Artist unknown
Late nineteenth century
Oil on cardboard
15 cm × 21.5 cm
(6 ins × 8½ ins)
Mr Roger Bichard

84 *The Country Fete*
Artist unknown
c. 1800
Oil on panel
a) 56 cm × 71 cm
(22 ins × 28 ins)
b) 56 cm × 71 cm
(22 ins × 28 ins)
Mr and Mrs Andras Kalman

85 *South View of Fen End Farm*
'M.S.L.'
'20th August 1790'
Watercolour on paper
25.5 cm × 40.5 cm
(10 ins × 16 ins)
Mr and Mrs Andras Kalman

86 *William Buckenham, Linen
Manufacturer's Cart*
Artist unknown
Early nineteenth century
Oil on canvas
33 cm × 40 cm
(13 ins × 15¾ ins)
Norwich City Museums

87 *Stagecoach Arriving at the White
Lion*
Artist unknown
Early nineteenth century
Oil on canvas
27.9 cm × 44.4 cm
(11 ins × 17½ ins)
Rutland Gallery, London

88– *Four Country Houses*
91 Artist unknown
c. 1840
Oil on canvas
44.4 cm × 66 cm each
(17½ ins × 26 ins)
Rutland Gallery, London

92 *The Earth Stopper*
George Smart
Second quarter of the
nineteenth century
Fabric collage on paper with
watercolour
25 cm × 37 cm
(10 ins × 14¾ ins)
Judkyn/Pratt

93 *City Foulers Mark*
Artist unknown
c. 1750
Oil on board
37 cm × 44.5 cm
(14½ ins × 17½ ins)
Mr and Mrs Andras Kalman

BIRDS AND BEASTS

94 *Adam Naming the Birds and
Beasts*
Artist unknown
First half of the nineteenth
century
Painted tin tray

55 cm × 76 cm
(20¾ ins × 30 ins)
Judkyn/Pratt

95 *The Lion Tamer*
W. H. Rogers
Mid nineteenth century
Oil on canvas
28 cm × 37 cm
(11 ins × 14½ ins)
Mr and Mrs Andras Kalman

96 *'Crib'; A Sporting Dog*
Thomas Roebuck
1860
Oil on canvas
73.5 cm × 94 cm
(29 ins × 37 ins)
Photograph Rutland Gallery,
London

97 *Canine Friends*
Artist unknown
Mid nineteenth century
Oil on canvas
33.5 cm × 40.5 cm
(13¼ ins × 16 ins)
Mr and Mrs Andras Kalman

98 *The Black Puppy*
Artist unknown
Early nineteenth century
Watercolour on velvet
17 cm × 19 cm
(6¾ ins × 7¾ ins)
Mr Ian McCallum

99 *The Kitten*
Artist unknown
Early nineteenth century
Watercolour on velvet
17 cm × 19.5 cm
(6¾ ins × 7¾ ins)
Mr Ian McCallum

100 *Feline Friends*
Artist unknown
Mid nineteenth century
Oil on canvas
33.5 cm × 40.5 cm
(13¼ ins × 16 ins)
Mr and Mrs Andras Kalman

101 *Cat and Kittens*
Artist unknown
Late nineteenth century
Oil on metal
24.1 cm × 34.3 cm
(9½ ins × 13½ ins)
Mr and Mrs Andras Kalman

102 *A Cat on a Cushion*
Artist unknown
Second half of the nineteenth
century
Embroidery on paper
15 cm × 20 cm
(6 ins × 8 ins)
Judkyn/Pratt

103 *A Cat among the Birds*
Artist unknown
Early eighteenth century
Oil on canvas
72.4 cm × 123.2 cm
(28½ ins × 48½ ins)
Photograph Rutland Gallery,
London

104 *The Miners' Canaries*
F. (or J.) Hodgson
1901
Back-painted glass
73.5 cm × 48 cm
(29 ins × 19 ins)
Mr Roger Bichard

105 *The Parrot*
Artist unknown
Eighteenth century
Silk, paper and mica
18.5 cm × 23 cm
(7¼ ins × 9 ins)
Mr and Mrs Michael Reeves

106 *Longhorn Cow*
Artist unknown
Early nineteenth century
Oil on canvas
38 cm × 47 cm
(15 ins × 18½ ins)
Museum of English Rural
Life, Reading

107 *Captain Scarlet*
Joseph Sheppard (1834–1928)
1865–70

Watercolour on paper
16.5 cm × 12 cm
(6½ ins × 4¾ ins)
Woodspring Museum,
Weston-super-Mare

108 *Daisy the Cow with her Calf*
Artist unknown
Early nineteenth century
Oil on board
56 cm × 71 cm
(22 ins × 28 ins)
Mr and Mrs Andras Kalman

109 *A Durham Shorthorn Bull with
Sheep*
Thomas Roebuck
1860
Oil on canvas
63.5 cm × 76.2 cm
(25 ins × 30 ins)
Rutland Gallery, London

110 *The Prize Ram*
Artist unknown
c. 1850
Oil on canvas
39.5 cm × 49.5 cm
(15½ ins × 19½ ins)
Mr and Mrs Andras Kalman

111 *The White Ewe*
William Bagshaw of Rugby
1846
Oil on canvas
45.5 cm × 66.5 cm
(18 ins × 26¼ ins)
Mr and Mrs Andras Kalman

112 *The White Ram*
William Bagshaw of Rugby
1846
Oil on canvas
45.5 cm × 66.5 cm
(18 ins × 26¼ ins)
Mr and Mrs Andras Kalman

113 *The Thorney Prize Ox*
James Clark
1858
Oil on canvas
56 cm × 66 cm
(22 ins × 26 ins)
Museum of English Rural
Life, Reading

114 *The Coach Horse*
Artist unknown
Early nineteenth century
Oil on canvas
38.5 cm × 41 cm
   (15 ins × 23 ins)
Photograph Rutland Gallery,
   London

115 *A Farmer with Prize Bull*
Artist unknown
c. 1830
Oil on canvas
43 cm × 66 cm
   (17 ins × 26 ins)
Photograph Rutland Gallery,
   London

116 *Prize Bull and Prize Cabbage*
W. Williams
1804
Oil on board
35 cm × 82.5 cm
   (13¾ ins × 32½ ins)
Mr and Mrs Andras Kalman

117 *A Farmer and Prize Heifer*
Artist unknown
Early nineteenth century
Oil on canvas
59 cm × 72 cm
   (23¼ ins × 28½ ins)
Mr and Mrs Andras Kalman

118 *Gloucestershire Old Spot Pig*
J. Miles of Northleach
1834
Oil on canvas
44.5 cm × 58.5 cm
   (17½ ins × 23½ ins)
Collection: City Museum
   and Art Gallery, Gloucester

119 *A Berkshire Pig: A Prize at*
   RAS Cardiff 1872
Richard Whitford ('Animal
   Painter to the Queen')
1872
Oil on canvas
38 cm × 43.5 cm
   (13¼ ins × 17¼ ins)
Museum of English Rural
   Life, Reading

THE SEA

120 *Scarborough*
Artist unknown
Early nineteenth century
Oil on canvas
55.5 cm × 84 cm
   (21¾ ins × 33 ins)
Mr and Mrs Andras Kalman

121 *A Yacht Race at Whitehaven*
Artist unknown
1795
Oil on canvas
52 cm × 72 cm
   (20½ ins × 28¼ ins)
Mr and Mrs Andras Kalman

122 *The William Miles of Bristol*
Signed 'Walters'
1827
Oil on canvas
47 cm × 79.5 cm
   (18½ ins × 31¼ ins)
City of Bristol, Museum and
   Art Gallery

123 *The Seahorse of 33 Guns*
Artist unknown
Early nineteenth century
Oil on cardboard
54.5 cm × 84 cm
   (21½ ins × 33 ins)
Judkyn/Pratt

124 *The Lowestoft Lifeboat*
J. Starling
c. 1860–70
Oil on canvas
43.2 cm × 66 cm
   (17 ins × 26 ins)
Mr and Mrs Andras Kalman

125 *The Fleet Off-shore*
Artist unknown
Last quarter of eighteenth
   century
Oil on panel
41 cm × 165 cm
   (16¼ ins × 65 ins)
Mr and Mrs Andras Kalman

126 *Admiral Rodney defeating the*
   French fleet of 35 sail under

Vice Admiral Comte de
Grasse off Dominica, 12 April
1782
Artist unknown
Late eighteenth century
Oil on canvas
77.5 cm × 174 cm
   (30½ ins × 68½ ins)
Private collection

127 *HMS Queen*
Artist unknown
'May 24, 1851'
Woolwork
58.5 cm × 73.5 cm
   (23 ins × 29 ins)
Judkyn/Pratt

128 *HMS Serapis*
Artist unknown
Mid nineteenth century
Woolwork
50 cm × 67.5 cm
   (19¾ ins × 26½ ins)
Mr and Mrs Andras Kalman

129 *Ships in an Estuary*
Artist unknown
Mid nineteenth century
Woolwork
43 cm × 69 cm
   (17 ins × 27¼ ins)
Judkyn/Pratt

130 *A Foreign Port*
Artist unknown
Mid nineteenth century
Oil on canvas
48.3 cm × 63.5 cm
   (19 ins × 25 ins)
Rutland Gallery, London

131 *The Yacht Sunbeam in the*
   Solent
Gunner G. Baldie of the
   Royal Artillery
c. 1850
Woolwork
59 cm × 61 cm
   (23¼ ins × 24 ins)
Mr and Mrs Andras Kalman

132 *Resurrection*
Elizabeth S. Gillard
'May 30th 1834'
Embroidery on silk with
    watercolour
39.5 cm × 34.5 cm
    ($15\frac{1}{2}$ ins × $13\frac{1}{2}$ ins)
Judkyn/Pratt

133 *Blessed are the Meek*
Artist unknown
Second half of the nineteenth
    century
Collage of butterflies on board
    with oil paint and sand
71 cm × 101.5 cm
    (28 ins × 40 ins)
Mr and Mrs Michael Reeves

134 *A Blind Beggar Being Led by a*
    Child
Artist unknown
Early nineteenth century
Pin-prick and watercolour
24.5 cm × 19.5 cm
    ($9\frac{3}{4}$ ins × $7\frac{3}{4}$ ins)
Tunbridge Wells Museum

135 *The Beggar – 'Pray Give a Trifle'*
Artist unknown
Early nineteenth century
Pin-prick and watercolour
24.5 cm × 19.5 cm
    ($9\frac{3}{4}$ ins × $7\frac{3}{4}$ ins)
Tunbridge Wells Museum

136 *Pedestrians with a Crossing*
    Sweeper
'Miss Gimbler'
'AD 1865'
Feltwork relief in wood
    shadow box
45 cm × 63.5 cm × 9 cm
    (18 ins × 25 ins × $3\frac{1}{2}$ ins)
Judkyn/Pratt

137 *Cranmer in his Study*
R. Brooke
1817
Wood and silk set in a
    shellwork pavilion and
    housed in a shadow box

34 cm × 37 cm × 15 cm
    ($13\frac{1}{2}$ ins × $14\frac{1}{2}$ ins × 6 ins)
Judkyn/Pratt

138 *An Old Man and an Old*
    Woman outside a House
Artist unknown
Late eighteenth century
Seed picture in contemporary
    shadow box
14 cm × 17.5 cm × 5 cm
    ($5\frac{1}{2}$ ins × 7 ins × 2 ins)
Judkyn/Pratt

139 *Old Bright, the Postman*
George Smart
1833
Feltwork collage on paper
    with watercolour
27.5 cm × 21 cm
    ($10\frac{3}{4}$ ins × $8\frac{1}{4}$ ins)
Mr and Mrs Andras Kalman

140 *Old Bright, the Postman*
George Smart
Early nineteenth century
Feltwork on sugar paper
    ground
29.5 cm × 32.5 cm
    ($11\frac{1}{2}$ ins × $12\frac{3}{4}$ ins)
Judkyn/Pratt

141 *Elizabeth Horne, the Goose Woman*
George Smart
Early nineteenth century
Feltwork collage on paper
    with watercolour
26 cm × 20 cm
    ($10\frac{1}{4}$ ins × $7\frac{3}{4}$ ins)
Judkyn/Pratt

142 George Smart's trade label
Printed by Clifford of
    Tunbridge Wells
Early nineteenth century
19.5 cm × 9 cm
    ($7\frac{1}{2}$ ins × $3\frac{1}{2}$ ins)
Judkyn/Pratt

143 *A Present from India*
'J. Wackett 4th Battalion
    Rifle Brigade'
Mid nineteenth century
Woolwork

33.5 cm × 33 cm
    ($13\frac{3}{4}$ ins × 13 ins)
Mr Ian McCallum

144 *The Scottish Girl*
George Smart
Early nineteenth century
Feltwork collage on paper
    with watercolour
27.5 cm × 22.5 cm
    (11 ins × $8\frac{3}{4}$ ins)
Tunbridge Wells Museum

145 *The Hussar*
George Smart
Early nineteenth century
Feltwork collage on paper
    with watercolour
27.5 cm × 22.5 cm
    (11 ins × $8\frac{3}{4}$ ins)
Tunbridge Wells Museum

146 *Min Don, Colwyn Bay*
Artist unknown
c. 1850
Straw work and gouache on paper
46.5 cm × 59 cm
    ($18\frac{1}{2}$ ins × $23\frac{1}{4}$ ins)
Judkyn/Pratt

147 *Goatherd with Goats*
Mrs Jane West
1838
Cut paper
18 cm × 30.5 cm
    (7 ins × 12 ins)
Blaise Castle House Folk
    Museum, Henbury, Bristol

148 *Cut Paper Trees*
Mary Loveday
1844
Cut paper
31 cm × 38 cm
    ($12\frac{1}{4}$ ins × 15 ins)
Luton Museum and Art Gallery

149 *Patchwork Bedcover*
James Williams of Wrexham
1842–52
Pieced cloth
305 cm × 274 cm
    (120 ins × 108 ins)
Welsh Folk Museum, St
    Fagans, Cardiff

Index

Numbers in italics refer to illustrations